Dr. Caroline Sakai is a picture o̶ *her patients. This book describes her unconventional ways that yields uncommon results even in the most difficult cases. The examples in this book speak for themselves. Thought Field Therapy (TFT) is a missing piece that may be applicable in just about everyone's life including your own. The techniques are simple yet powerful and useful for conditions from simple habit change to full-blown PTSD.*

—Terry Shintani, MD, JD MPH, Founding President, Hawaii Health Foundation

Never before have I experienced such highly inspirational dedication and warmth as that which shines through Dr. Caroline Sakai's work with Thought Field Therapy. Her stories of Rwanda's genocide survivors show the ultimate level of compassion and love for your fellow human beings. This method is easy to learn, apply, and so empowering!

—Rev. Deacon Debra Nalani'ikaleomana, New University of Hawaii

Overcoming Adversity is a vital informational and training asset to helping laypersons and professionals assist with possible strategies that can help heal.

—Carole G. Stern, RN, DCEP, Past President, Association for Comprehensive Energy Psychology (ACEP)

Energy psychology combines modern methods for overcoming trauma with ancient techniques for healing the body. The mixture is powerful. Survivors of traumas overcome the experiences that have shattered their psyches. In the past, after such trauma, survivors often spent the remainder of their lives in the nightmarish terror of PTSD, unable to rebuild their lives beyond a dark shadow of what had been. With energy psychology, they heal, and they rebuild their lives with surging creativity, confidence, and deep compassion for others who are struggling....This book tells their stories. You cannot read it without being transformed.

—David Feinstein, PhD, Author of *Ethics Handbook for Energy Healing Practitioners*

Overcoming Adversity

How Energy Tapping Transforms Your Life's Worst Experiences

A Primer for Posttraumatic Growth

by Caroline E. Sakai, PhD
Foreword by David Feinstein, PhD

www.EnergyPsychologyPress.com

Energy Psychology Press
3340 Fulton Rd., #442, Fulton, CA 95439
www.EnergyPsychologyPress.com

Overcoming Adversity
How Energy Tapping Tranforms Your Life's Worst Experiences

Cataloging-in-Publication Data

Overcoming adversity / by Caroline Sakai
    p. cm.
ISBN 978-1-60415-247-0
1. Post-traumatic stress disorder—Treatment. 2. Psychic trauma—Treatment. 3. Psychotherapy. I. Sakai, Caroline.
RCC552.P67C73 2014
616.85'21-dc21

© 2014 Caroline E. Sakai

Cover design by Victoria Valentine
Editing by Stephanie Marohn
Typesetting by Karin Kinsey
Photos by Gary Quinn
Typeset in ITC Galliard and Mona Lisa Solid ITC
Printed in USA by Bang Printing
First Edition

10 9 8 7 6 5 4 3 2 1

Important note: While Energy Psychology has produced remarkable clinical results, it must still be considered to be in the experimental stage and thus practitioners and the public must take complete responsibility for their use of it. Readers are strongly cautioned and advised to consult with a physician, psychologist, psychiatrist, or other licensed health care professional before utilizing any of the information in this book. The information is based on information from sources believed to be accurate and reliable and every reasonable effort has been made to make the information as complete and accurate as possible, but such completeness and accuracy cannot be guaranteed and is not guaranteed.

The author, publisher, and contributors to this book, and their successors, assigns, licensees, employees, officers, directors, attorneys, agents, and other parties related to them (a) do not make any representations, warranties, or guarantees that any of the information will produce any particular medical, psychological, physical, or emotional result; (b) are not engaged in the rendering of medical, psychological or other advice or services; (c) do not provide diagnosis, care, treatment, or rehabilitation of any individual; and (d) do not necessarily share the views and opinions expressed in the information. The information has not undergone evaluation and testing by the United States Food and Drug Administration or similar agency of any other country and is not intended to diagnose, treat, prevent, mitigate, or cure any disease. Risks that might be determined by such testing are unknown. If the reader purchases any services or products as a result of the information, the reader or user acknowledges that the reader or user has done so with informed consent. The information is provided on an "as is" basis without any warranties of any kind, express or implied, whether warranties as to use, merchantability, fitness for a particular purpose, or otherwise.

The author, publisher, and contributors to this book, and their successors, assigns, licensees, employees, officers, directors, attorneys, agents, and other parties related to them (a) expressly disclaim any liability for and shall not be liable for any loss or damage including but not limited to use of the information; (b) shall not be liable for any direct or indirect compensatory, special, incidental, or consequential damages or costs of any kind or character; (c) shall not be responsible for any acts or omissions by any party including but not limited to any party mentioned or included in the information or otherwise; (d) do not endorse or support any material or information from any party mentioned or included in the information or otherwise; and (e) will not be liable for damages or costs resulting from any claim whatsoever. The within limitation of warranties may be limited by the laws of certain states and/or other jurisdictions and so some of the foregoing limitations may not apply to the reader who may have other rights that vary from state to state. If the reader or user does not agree with any of the terms of the foregoing, the reader or user should not use the information in this book or read it. A reader who continues reading this book will be deemed to have accepted the provisions of this disclaimer.

Please consult qualified health practitioners regarding your use of Thought Field Therapy (TFT), Emotional Freedom Techniques (EFT), and other forms of Energy Psychology.

Contents

Part I—Stories of Recovery and Resilience

Depression

Fear/Panic

Stress/Anxiety

Anger/Rage

Trauma

Complex Issues

Foreword

When Dr. Sakai sent me the manuscript for this book, she shared the following story, which had just come her way. It describes one of the many reverberations of her having helped bring Thought Field Therapy, the original form of Energy Psychology, to Rwanda.

One of the policemen we trained has been highly successful in using TFT to help reduce domestic violence, murders, and suicides in his precinct. Because the community had learned to trust and revere him, they cooperated with his investigations, and he sent many criminals to prison. Such successes can create enemies. It came to pass that he was eventually falsely accused and imprisoned. That can be a death sentence for a policeman. Policemen are often sent to the same prisons as the people they originally arrested. Many policemen have, while awaiting trial, been murdered by angry, violent prisoners who remember them from the other side of the badge. The policeman felt terror on learning he was being sent where many inmates would kill him the first chance they got. To get a handle on his fear, he applied TFT to himself. He physically tapped the TFT fear points on his body. His anxiety melted, and pretty soon, he found himself laughing.

He continued to tap, using different TFT sequences for whatever difficult emotions might arise for him in his new, highly dangerous home. Prisons do not allow a great deal of privacy, and one of the prisoners (not one of those he'd sent to prison), seeing him tapping and appearing to be at such peace—even joyful, asked him what he was doing. He showed him, and the prisoner started tapping and laughing too. Soon, more prisoners were curious, and the policeman taught each of them. Word spreads quickly in a prison. Before long, many of the prisoners and staff were tapping and feeling peace and joy. Everyone knew the danger the policeman was in, and they protected him from the prisoners who were eager for revenge. Eventually, one of the prisoners he had arrested wanted to know what he was doing, and the policeman showed him the TFT sequence for intense anger. The man's rage toward the policeman evaporated. Soon, all the prisoners, even those he had put into prison, were tapping away, as were the staff.

After 3 months, the policeman's trial came up. He was cleared of any wrongdoing. But he realized he had been sent to prison for an important reason. He now goes with the priests into the prisons to teach TFT tapping.

I am honored to be asked to write this foreword to *Overcoming Adversity: How Energy Tapping Transforms Your Life's Worst Experiences* for the woman who has been the catalyst for hundreds of stories, known and unknown, of remarkable human courage and triumph in the face of emotional devastation. This book is a beautiful record of the experiences of a psychologist who has crossed the boundaries of conventional psychotherapy and crossed the boundaries of national borders to bring the most effective tools psychology has developed to those who have suffered unimaginable disasters.

Energy psychology combines modern methods for overcoming trauma with ancient techniques for healing the body. The mixture is powerful. Survivors of traumas overcome the experiences that have shattered their psyches. In the past, after such trauma, survivors often spent the remainder of their lives in the nightmarish terror of PTSD, unable to rebuild their lives beyond a dark shadow of what had been. With Energy Psychology, they heal, and they rebuild their lives with surging creativity, confidence, and deep compassion for others who are struggling.

Dr. Sakai has carefully observed their journeys from emotional impairment to a blossoming of the spirit. She has identified four stages in optimal healing, resilience, and growth, with personal healing being perhaps the largest challenge but just the first stage. Beyond their own healing, the people she has worked with also find forgiveness, gratitude, and, finally, fulfillment through service. This book tells their stories. You cannot read it without being transformed.

—David Feinstein, PhD
Ashland, Oregon

Acknowledgments

The inspiration for this book came from the thousands of brave men, women, children, and adolescents who have rebounded from trauma and adversity and who have gone the extraordinary mile to give back to others with their appreciation, care, enthusiasm for life, forgiveness, and efforts to make a difference in their lives and the lives of others. I will be ever in awe of their courage, perseverance, and resilience and filled with gratitude for the gifts of insight, knowledge, and wisdom they brought to me on their journey to living with peace, joy, and gratitude.

I am grateful to my daughter, Stephanie, for her artistic, technical, and emotional support and encouragement in putting together this book. Dr. Marvin Mathews, Greg Payton, Greg Tanida, Dr. David Paperny, and Dr. James McKoy were early stalwart supporters of this new approach that was initially made available to clients who were, with conventional approaches, struggling with little to no relief from their pain and suffering.

My appreciation goes to Dr. Paul Oas (who initiated my involvement in Rwanda), Father Jean Marie Vianney Dushimiyimana, Father Augustin Nzabonimana, Bishop Servilien Nzakamwita, Pastor Celestin Mitabu, Dr. Peter Ilunga, Darling Clementine, Prosper Ishimwe, Gary and Cyndie Quinn, Dr. David Feinstein, Drs. Ann and Ken Yabusaki, Dr. Dawson Church, Suzanne Connolly, Robin Rohr, Alan Shinn, Dr. Judy Daniels, Dr. Michael D'Andrea, Debra Nalaniikaleomana New, all who have consented to share their disguised case histories, all the therapists trained in Rwanda and the thousands they have helped, and all the Energy Psychology volunteer practitioners who are helping to make a difference in healing hurts in the world. And my deep appreciation goes to the late Dr. Roger Callahan for his development of TFT and paving the way for Energy Psychology.

Overcoming Adversity is dedicated to all the Rwandans who have transformed my life and inspired me to share their amazing stories of resilience, which could in turn inspire others. Part of the proceeds from sales of this book will be going to support them in their healing of their nation and people.

Introduction

Overcoming Adversity:
A Path to Health and Resilience

We must become the change we want to see in the world.

—Mahatma Gandhi

Most of us in the Western world feel our daily stress levels rising. We have more responsibilities and things to take care of than we have time for in a day. Stress lowers immune function, which affects the body's ability to protect, restore, and heal itself. We sleep less, eat processed food, and most of us don't make the time for daily exercise. We then rely on pills to fix the markedly increasing ills that we foster with this highly stressful and unhealthy lifestyle. However, pills, even when they help, tend to suppress or mask the symptoms we have and don't necessarily treat the underlying causes of the problem.

We can regain control of our lives and our health, however. The way to do this begins with learning to boost the body's ability to heal itself. Using Thought Field Therapy (TFT) and other Energy Psychology methods, we can overcome anxiety, anger, depression, fear, pain, phobias, traumas, and more. TFT is a treatment that is, in fact, self-administered, using meridian acupoints (specified acupuncture points) to lessen or remit the symptoms of trauma or other psychological distresses, thus being readily accessible, always available, and self-controlled. It offers profound benefits for healing outside the confines of typical medical settings. Energy tapping can help all of us improve our everyday lives, as can be seen in the following examples.

Trisha had been unable to drive since the car she was driving was T-boned by a van going through a red light. She cringed and clenched her teeth and fists and had cramps from tension in her legs and abdomen when she was a passenger and often startled the driver with her screams of fright as she perceived danger at every turn. Trisha's physical injuries had long healed but the posttrauma flashbacks and nightmares were entrapping her and restricting her mobility and life. She was elated at doors opening for her again after she tapped through her trauma, and her hypervigilance, hyper-startle (exaggerated startle response), and hyperreactivity calmed down so that she could ride a car without unnerving the driver. After continuing her protocols for a month, Trisha triumphed over her trauma and got behind the wheel and drove herself.

Darren found his life constricting with the nagging chronic pain in his shoulder, neck, and lower back. He got some relief through his chiropractic adjustments and physical therapy exercises, but he was no longer able to tolerate the side effects of his pain medications. Decades ago, he had been active in several sports. Now it was painful watching these sports on TV. Darren found himself becoming more isolated as he avoided events that entailed sitting for long periods of time. Eventually, he even gave up going for walks. With tapping sequences to help him manage his pain, Darren has been able to resume a more active life, and is now back on a healthy living path.

Mabel had trouble keeping focused on what she was doing, as she kept worrying about the "what ifs" of the future, and also ruminating and kicking herself with regrets about the past. Mabel didn't concentrate on what she was doing sufficiently to remember sequences and details, which led to her getting exasperated at her-self, and worrying about losing her mind and memory. She finally felt her prayers were answered when she found she could literally tap her oppressive worrying down. As her mind calmed and her body relaxed, Mabel was surprised that she could see her problems in clearer perspective, develop solutions more effectively, and follow through on decisions without her typical vacillations, indecisiveness, and self-doubts.

Daphne never seemed content or satisfied with anything or anyone. She was too easily irritated and annoyed, and was in a perennially low mood. She snapped at people who expressed concern, and almost rudely rejected offers of help. She often kept to herself to avoid having run-ins and conflicts. Daphne spent a lot of time sleeping but woke up feeling even more tired. She often skipped meals because she was asleep or too angry to eat, but she ate sugary, fried, or other high-calorie, low-nutrition foods. Daphne and her family and friends were astonished when she was calmer and actually civil after several Energy Psychology tapping protocols. Daphne helped herself to increased tolerance, higher energy, better mood, and improved social relationships.

Phyllis shrieked and dropped whatever she was holding when a cockroach scampered or flew into her view. She ran out of the room and would not go back in until someone came to find and exterminate the roach. Phyllis knew her reactions were extreme, but nothing she had tried could allay her fears. Friends who said she was being silly to be so afraid of a little insect made her feel bad about herself. She burst into tears of relief and joy when she tapped her phobia away, and felt proud of herself when she even got rid of a cockroach all by herself.

Abigail went into rages and tirades that created constant drama and trauma in her interpersonal life. She seemed to wake up angry, and what others might consider minor issues set off firestorms of outrage. Family and acquaintances were fearful of incurring her wrath, so they often spoke softly and tentatively. Unfortunately, she then more frequently misunderstood what was being said and made assumptions that set off her verbal venom. Abigail learned to balance herself internally, and found she could take time-outs to tap down her anger and rage. She also could ground herself and keep herself stable at a lower threshold by using Energy Psychology to prevent or ameliorate problems that could be anticipated.

As a psychologist for many years and now additionally as a trainer and practitioner of Energy Psychology, I have discovered four major principles for overcoming debilitating stresses and traumas to optimize healing and growth. We can not only recover and heal from traumas and adversities, but we can also become stronger, more resilient, and better equipped to optimize our potentials through posttraumatic growth. This can empower us to have the options to reach and grow beyond ourselves, and attain the highest of life's satisfactions and joys, by being able to be of service helping others.

The Four Principles for Optimizing Healing, Resilience, and Growth

1. Healing Damages, Wounds, or Hurts

The first step for anyone who is suffering from impairing mental, emotional, or physical pain is to heal the untreated traumas, hurts, and psychological wounds that can manifest in a magnitude of ways. Efforts to manage or contain that pain can take over our energy, focus, and direction. TFT is well suited as a self-treatment that can be utilized by the individual any time and any place, as needed to lessen the gamut of emotional distresses. The stories and examples that I'll share in the eight main sections of this book (from Depression to Large-Scale Trauma) include a cross-section of case applications of TFT with generalizations of their treatment protocols outlined at the end of each chapter.

2. Moving Past Resentments to Resilience

Once the negative emotions are addressed and processed and no longer flood the individual with debilitating or engulfing disturbances, it is easier to be more objective. The defensive and protective barriers are opened up, and others' perspectives and points of view become more visible and comprehensible. The doorway to moving onward, and even to possible forgiveness where personally appropriate and feasible, may then begin to open. Prior hurts and emotional pains often surface along with the thoughts, beliefs, and attitudes that have developed over time, perhaps in reaction to these experiences. We may need to process through many layers of negative onslaughts to a sense of worth and well-being before it is possible to simply experience the present moments without the painful haunting of the past.

People can become trapped by their past experiences and beliefs. It's like being a broken record stuck on intensely negative experiences that loop around in the parts of the brain that control mood and memory. In surviving trauma, a person may cope by retreating from others and rejecting their overtures, lashing out defensively, or blaming and over-reacting to current people and situations, influenced by what the person endured in the past although with different people and circumstances.

Once the disturbances are removed as thoroughly and completely as is practical and feasible, the door is opened to the healing step of taking responsibility for our contributions to conflicts or problems, making appropriate amends and restitutions when needed, and moving into a place of forgiving others and ourselves. Eventually, we feel more at peace within, with significant others, and with the world around us. We can then use peak-performance procedures to grow stronger and ever more resilient, and to enhance our self-confidence and positive behaviors.

3. Optimizing Health and Gratitude

When we are free from traumas, resentments, anger, anxiety, depression, and other negative states, we can begin to move from coping to thriving. When we shift our psychical and emotional equilibrium, we discover a surge of energy that moves us into our optimal and maximal well-being. Our energy is widely available then to keep us in our optimal healthy state, our highest immunological level of functioning. In a place of emotional health, we can think clearer and kinder thoughts. We can move and exercise more robustly and regularly. We can attain our goals, and we can feel at peace within ourselves and in our relationships and interactions with others. We can thrive with optimal health and resilience, and more fully experience life with the grace of gratitude.

4. Attaining Fulfillment Through Service

The greatest joy of all is using our talents, skills, and gifts to help others or humanitarian causes—to participate in and embrace meaningful service to others. The maximal actualization of ourselves is facilitated most profoundly by what we can do to help humanity, using all the knowledge, skill, creativity, and ingenuity we possess and attaining maximal living—a life of high purpose and profound meaning.

I have seen people overcome their adversities and become free of the constraints that limit their abilities. They are then able to have more meaningful interactions and connections with people in their lives. It is possible to move upward into the realm of actualizing our highest potential, and we may be inspired to serve in new ways that enhance the lives of others who are less fortunate or who are devastated by trauma and adversity. We can kindle or reactivate the joy and elation of being of service to help ourselves, help others, and be in tune with our higher power.

How I Discovered TFT

I came across TFT quite by accident. For over 45 years, I have been working as a licensed clinical psychologist and social worker. My chief reason for choosing this field for my life's work was to help people who suffered from debilitating conditions so they could get back on their feet and lead happier, more productive lives.

For 31 years, I served at Kaiser Behavioral Health Services in Hawaii and also for a few years in California, and had the opportunity to work with a broad spectrum of symptoms and disorders. As chief psychologist, I was privileged to supervise other therapists, confer with psychiatrists and medical doctors, innovate and develop needed programs, and treat the most complex and challenging clients. I have traveled to study with master therapists and leading practitioners of the major treatment modalities over the decades, including Salvador Minuchin, Aaron Beck, Donald Meichenbaum, Marizio Andolfi, Christine Padeski, Jeffrey Zeig, Cloe Madanes, Francine Shapiro, and many others. All have been very helpful with specific aspects of circumscribed problems with selected people. As chief psychologist at Kaiser Behavioral Health Services, I saw that all therapists of different orientations encountered some challenging situations that were not appreciably improved by the traditional psycho-therapy modalities.

In developing an integrated behavioral medicine program to facilitate easier access and more rapid treatment of mind-body issues right in the medical clinics, I searched for more tools that we could use to help people to health more rapidly. This search for alternative modalities of treatment in the literature led me to an article by Dr. Charles Figley and Dr. Joyce Carbonnell on promising new approaches. Of special interest to me was Thought Field Therapy, with which I was not familiar but which looked extremely promising. I discovered that there was a family of similar Energy Psychology modalities that had branched out from TFT. I elected to learn from the originator of these Energy Psychology approaches, Dr. Roger Callahan.

I personally experienced unexpected improvements in my physical health as I used TFT to improve my immune function and help with my lifelong struggle with systemic lupus erythematosus. TFT helped remit symptoms and eliminate the physical pains. I was astounded at the results obtained and continued to study with Dr. Callahan to learn all levels of TFT. Although formal research studies were lacking then, the ease of use, rapidity of results, and lack of negative side effects made it attractive to use to lower distress and suffering. Initially, I thought it would primarily serve as psychological first aid until more in-depth treatments could be accessed as needed. To my surprise, many people needed no further treatment. Those who needed further treatment could then also work more rapidly with conventional approaches, with enhanced results.

After seeing TFT work on a personal level and a clinic-wide level, it became clear that TFT could be used to improve community health and could certainly be effective in facilitating recovery in large-scale trauma. This led to my participation in ATFT (Association for TFT) Foundation trauma-relief deployments to New Orleans post-Katrina and subsequently to Rwanda to work with genocide survivors.

And that brings me to the reason for writing this book. Seeing the successful implementation of TFT in helping communities heal from large-scale trauma, I wrote this book to make this invaluable method accessible to as many people as possible. Energy psychology can maximize and optimize people's functioning levels and health, improve enjoyment of life, enhance relationships, improve productivity, elevate resilience, stimulate altruistic growth, reduce health-care costs, and even improve the well-being of our communities.

How to Use This Book

Overcoming Adversity provides an introduction to TFT and Energy Psychology, including some of the key research demonstrating its impact, and summarizes basic instructions so that you can learn this method. The appendices provide detailed information about the different TFT protocols.

Chapters 2 through 19 (Part I) tell the compelling stories of some of the thousands of brave women, men, children, and adolescents who have rebounded from trauma and adversity to give back to others and make a difference in their lives. All the cases are true; however, the client names and certain details have been changed to protect identities. These individual cases are organized by the most common concerns I encounter in my daily practice. It is important to note, however, that no one comes to my practice with only one symptom. Though I have organized these sections based on specific problems, each case includes various symptoms that the client had to work through. Part II shares the details of TFT in my work with Rwandan survivors to exemplify how powerful this method is. (Note: A portion of the proceeds from this book will go to the Izere Center in Byumba, Rwanda, to support their healing missions helping fellow Rwandans across their country.)

No matter what we have gone through in life, we can all improve our current state of health. Some of the people featured in the case histories had all but given up hope of leading a normal life. What they have in common is that, once they began to heal, they felt compelled to help others. Knowing that we can make a difference and that we each possess this capacity can help us to feel less victimized, less overwhelmed, more hopeful, and more empowered. And that can start us on the path of recovery and healing toward enhanced resilience and posttraumatic growth.

Whether you've come to this book in a state of despair about the unhappiness and struggle you've been living with, whether you have spent many months or years dealing with and overcoming personal demons and traumas but are looking for a way to feel more at peace and release the restrictions and struggles that follow you in life, or whether you are a health professional or advocate seeking ways to make the world a better place, I hope *Overcoming Adversity* will give you the inspiration and practical direction to make and be the change you wish to see and experience in the world.

1

Understanding Energy Psychology and Thought Field Therapy

A person's mind stretched to a new idea never goes back to its original dimensions.

—Oliver Wendell Holmes

We are on the verge of a revolution in harnessing energy for health and well-being. We can literally tap into internal mental and physical energy resources to help us heal, transform, and grow. The forerunner of the energy tapping methods is Thought Field Therapy (TFT), which was developed by psychologist Roger Callahan. Many variations have proliferated, and are collectively referred to as Energy Psychology.

TFT consists of activation of selected acupoints on the skin's surface, primarily through tapping or rubbing with the fingers, while focusing on the thought field (targeted emotion, trigger, symptom, or problem). The selected acupoints and the order in which they are tapped are specific to the thought field being addressed. Once learned, acupoint activation can also be done mentally through concentrated focusing on the acupoints in the prescribed order.

The selected acupoint sequence (called an "algorithm") for each thought field is determined through a diagnostic methodology using a systematic form of energy testing. This individualized diagnostic methodology requires training and practice to master, so it is taught in hands-on TFT diagnostic workshops by certified instructors. Standard TFT algorithms derived from the individualized treatments are taught in a number of workshops. The Association for Comprehensive Energy Psychology

(ACEP) certification trainings for practitioners also include parts of this methodology. Variants of this Energy Psychology method have emerged. The most widely known is Emotional Freedom Techniques (EFT), the standardized form of which is Clinical EFT, as described in the *Clinical EFT Handbook* (Church & Marohn, 2013).

General acupoint sequences that have been found to be helpful for 70–80% of the people with the symptoms by Callahan and others are presented in Appendix C. For readers with no experience with Energy Psychology, this book will introduce you to the realm of possibilities for self-care enhancement. Additional self-help books on Energy Psychology, DVDs, videos, and classes on the acupoint sequences are widely available. For further and deeper work with Energy Psychology, many practitioners are available for consultations and classes. Some of the resources for finding practitioners, classes, and training for Energy Psychology are listed in Appendix H.

For professionals who have experience with Energy Psychology, the techniques and case studies in this book can deepen your practice, add to your repertoire, and inspire you to bring this healing modality to communities that are in desperate need of healing.

As will be seen in many of the treatments in this book, the complexities of emotions can often be targeted by assessing the acupoints needed through the individualized diagnostic procedures, by using combinations of algorithms, or by treating the facets of the emotions serially. For example, trauma with anger and guilt can be addressed with a combined sequence, or the trauma can be treated initially, then the anger, and then the guilt.

Even babies, impaired elderly, and animals can benefit from TFT. Agitated babies have been soothed by gentle bilateral (on both sides of the body when feasible) massage by their parents on the acupoint sequences. Traumatized and frightened pets have been calmed by their veterinarians, trainers, or owners with comforting bilateral massage on the trauma treatment points. Distraught and confused elders have been reassured and stabilized by their caretakers administering the appropriate treatment with bilateral massaging of the acupoints when the elders are in the triggering situations. The bilateral massaging of acupoints in an algorithm sequence could provide a soothing and comforting physiological effect that simultaneously calms the emotional disturbance.

What Are Algorithms and Subjective Units of Distress?

An algorithm is like a treatment recipe of selected acupoints in a specific order. These treatment recipes emerged from TFT diagnostic testing of hundreds of people while they focused on a certain thought field (e.g., anger, panic, pain from a sore shoulder, an upsetting incident). The algorithm steps and the most commonly used algorithms are included in appendices B and C.

For those in clinical practice or doing research, the subjective units of distress (SUD) scale can be used to assess the progress of treatment, and to determine the next step on the decision tree of a treatment protocol. The SUD scale is a rating method developed by Joseph Wolpe (1958). A person rates the emotional intensity of a specific disturbance on a scale of 0 to 10 while focusing on the thought field in the present moment, with 0 indicating no distress and 10 indicating the highest level of distress for that thought field.

How Does Energy Psychology/TFT Work?

While focusing on specific distressing memories, targets, emotions, or symptoms, we tap or activate specific acupoints, and this activation appears to reduce the level of the stress hormone cortisol circulating in the body and to stimulate the body's natural healing and processing functions. A constant state of stress (physical, mental, and emotional) takes its toll on the body, with high stress leading to overstimulation of the sympathetic nervous system. Neuromuscular tension develops throughout the body. Cortisol levels rise and course through blood and tissues. Blood pressure elevates, nutrient and energy stores deplete, and immune function lowers. The body needs to be brought back into a state of balance by enhancing the parasympathetic functioning, which appears to be attained with the activation of specific acupoints.

The mechanism of action behind Energy Psychology's and specifically TFT's strong and rapid outcomes is in need of further systematic study. Functional MRI and other imaging studies at Harvard Medical School (Hui et al., 2000; Fang et al., 2009) have demonstrated that stimulating specific acupuncture points with needles produced decreases in activity in the amygdala, hippocampus, and other brain areas associated with fear. Daniel Cherkin and colleagues (2009) found that both acupuncture and simulated acupuncture (with sham needles without actual skin penetration) produced better results with chronic low back pain than conventional medical care. David Feinstein (2010) hypothesizes that the rapid results reported in treating anxiety-based disorders are because tapping on acupoints while focusing on disturbing memories or cues extinguishes the anxious response. Additional explanations are needed for the rapid reduction of other dysfunctional conditions and emotional responses.

What Is the Evidence for the Effectiveness of Energy Psychology/TFT?

Dr. David Feinstein (2012) conducted a comprehensive review of research on the efficacy of Energy Psychology (EP). He notes that EP approaches utilize established clinical methods such as exposure and cognitive restructuring and also incorporate stimulation of acupuncture points accompanying the activation of targeted psychological issues. Feinstein's literature review covers 51 studies, including 18 randomized controlled trials (RCTs). He concluded that the strong effect sizes and positive statistical results across the 18 RCTs far exceeded chance after relatively few EP sessions.

An RCT of Emotional Freedom Techniques by Church, Yount, and Brooks (2012) found significant decreases in cortisol levels using salivary cortisol assays, along with decreases in anxiety and depression symptoms. In a study of EFT using electroencephalography (ECT), Lambrou, Pratt, and Chevalier (2003) found significant reduction in anxiety symptoms and muscle tension, and normalized theta brain-wave activity.

The following are summaries of randomized controlled and uncontrolled outcome studies specifically on TFT.

Suzanne Connolly and I (Connolly & Sakai, 2011) investigated randomization to TFT treatment or wait-list control with 145 adult genocide survivors in Kigali, Rwanda, and found significant differences between pre- and posttreatment scores on two translated, standardized PTSD (posttraumatic stress disorder) self-inventories. The control group demonstrated significant improvements after they subsequently received the TFT treatment. At 2-year follow-up, improvements had held. A second randomized controlled study completed at Izere Center in Byumba, Rwanda (Connolly, Roe-Sepowitz, and Sakai, 2013) had similarly significant results.

We (Sakai, Connolly & Oas, 2010) also studied 50 of the highest scoring—on translated, standardized measures of PTSD rated by the students and their caretakers—of 188 adolescent genocide survivors pre- and posttreatment with TFT. Posttreatment, 94% no longer met PTSD criteria according to the caretaker ratings. Results were holding at 92% not meeting PTSD criteria at 1-year follow-up. One inspiring girl, who was 3 years old at the time of the genocide, had been haunted for a dozen years by intrusive, debilitating flashbacks and nightly nightmares of witnessing her entire family and relatives and neighbors brutally killed before her eyes. She was forlorn, depressed, and unable to focus and study in school, and felt hopeless. After one extensive treatment with TFT, she reported the traumatic memories fading into the distant past, her depression and hopelessness lifting, and fond memories emerging of her early pre-genocide childhood, and she smiled and laughed for the first time since the tragedies.

Carl Johnson and colleagues (2001) summarized their work with 105 torture survivors in Kosovo, reporting improvement in 103 survivors after treatment with TFT. Crystal Folkes (2002) found significant symptom reduction on a PTSD checklist with refugees after one to three TFT sessions. Beverly Schoninger and John Hartung (2010) reported significant reductions in self-reported public speaking anxiety after treatment with TFT. Peter Lambrou and colleagues (2003) found reduction in muscle tension and EEG activity improvement in treating claustrophobia. Kaiser Permanente (Hawaii) HMO's process evaluations (2001) of different applications of TFT are summarized in Appendix G.

Overall, investigations to date have demonstrated statistically significant results. Energy Psychology methods appear to be promising approaches to attaining significant reductions or remissions of emotional distress and psychological symptoms. Further research is needed, including studies that can demonstrate and clarify the exact mechanisms of action.

Can TFT Be Used with Other Therapies?

TFT can be readily integrated into cognitive therapy, behavioral therapy, anger management, and other traditional talk therapies and can enhance whatever effective means of treatment the clinician is practicing (Connolly, 2004). I have found TFT also works well with interpersonal therapy, Gestalt therapy, existential therapy, reality therapy, EMDR (Eye Movement Desensitization and Reprocessing), narrative therapy, skill-building methods, and psycho-educational approaches. TFT can be used as the primary or sole treatment, and it can also be integrated with and used to augment and speed the progress of other forms of therapy.

Are There Other Ways to Activate the Acupoints Besides Tapping?

Tapping on the acupoints is the easiest way for most people to stimulate the acupoints. With greater concentration, however, it can be done mentally. There are a number of circumstances in which mental tapping is necessary or preferable. We may choose to do the treatments mentally when in a public situation. Mental activation is essential for quadriplegic individuals and others with paralyses or impairments that preclude physical self-administration by tapping. Bilateral massage (gently rubbing both of each meridian acupoint needed—there are two of each point, one on each side of the body) is typically used with babies, animals, and elderly people who find massaging the points more soothing than tapping them. Touching and holding the acupoints while breathing is a variation used by John Diepold, Victoria Britt, and Sheila Bender (2004). Alternative acupoints along the meridians can be used when there is some difficulty in tapping the prescribed acupoints; these alternatives can be found on acupuncture meridian charts.

How Long Do the Effects Last?

The length of time that effects last in TFT depends on what is being treated. Phobias and completely treated traumas generally do not need retreatment. Completeness of treatment is essential for effects to hold over time. Some issues may require serial treatment sessions to work through multiple layers and complexities. With anxiety, anger, grief, and other emotions that can be set off by new circumstances or events, self-treatment can be used to manage the symptoms. Individualized energy sensitivities can set off symptoms; these sensitivities can be identified via the pulse test and log (see Appendix F) and individualized energy sensitivities testing. The individualized energy sensitivities should then be avoided where possible, as with the panic attack cases in chapters 5 and 6.

What Is the Goal in Overcoming Adversity?

The path of Overcoming Adversity takes us into the heart of individual and collective traumas and adversities, and shares the transformational healing steps of Energy Psychology's Thought Field Therapy. In rebounding from trauma, grief, and adversity, we are then able to develop deeper insights and internal resources and resilience, as well as grow and connect with others in more meaningful and caring ways. We are able not only to optimize our personal health and well-being, but also to actualize our highest potential and perhaps even inspire and help others maximize their functioning and lives.

Part I

Stories of Recovery and Resilience

DEPRESSION

2

A Life
Saved to Help Others

Whatever the mind can conceive and believe, it can achieve.

—Napoleon Hill

"Depression" is a word we hear a lot these days. Commercials for medication promising relief fill our television screens and magazines. Once never talked about, depression has come to the forefront in our culture. Stress, sleep deprivation, exhaustion, unhealthy eating habits, and chronic inactivity can lower our resistance to depression, which is like the common cold of mental health. Trauma, losses, chronic physical pain, prolonged rage and anger, unremitting resentment, and chronic anxiety can likewise leave us more vulnerable to depression. Depressive disorders affect an estimated 9–10% of the U.S. population. I see many clients who, if not currently, have at one time or another suffered from depression. If someone has been through a severe trauma, with the intense agitation and anxiety that often accompanies it, depression may follow at some stage in life.

Remarkably, some of these clients have been on antidepressant medication for years without robust results. Many are still unable to function fully and lead fulfilling and productive lives. I have seen TFT help people dealing with troubling depressive issues turn their lives around. TFT can help reduce the contributory issues, such as trauma, grief, anxiety, and stress, as well as ameliorate the lethargy, low energy, and feeling of hopelessness. In cases of severe depression and suicidal thoughts, TFT can be used in conjunction with psychiatric, psychological, medical, and social service interventions.

One particular client, Jake, had battled depression for years. Eventually, he gave in and tried to commit suicide. He was horrified when he woke from a coma and found that he had survived shooting himself through the mouth. He felt he had failed yet again. Miraculously, he recovered from the physical wounds, but the deep, dark depression hung around him like a suffocating veil. He had no joy, no will to live; and he was fearful and anxious, with panic episodes, haunting nightmares, and vivid memories of his troubled life.

He experienced early trauma as a youth placed in a residential facility for developmental disabilities because of his dyslexia. Jake was not allowed to see his parents for the first 2 weeks to allow time to orient and adjust to the residential program. During this time, he was beaten for not doing things correctly. His parents were unaware of this horrific treatment. Being terrified and having nowhere to turn for help, he started to wet his bed. Sadly, he was beaten more for this. By the time his parents came to visit, he was anxious, depressed, and withdrawn. They were shocked at his deteriorated state but didn't understand what had happened.

Jake was further traumatized when he was kidnapped later in his youth. Understandably, he became even more apprehensive and fearful. By then he began experiencing full-blown depression. He had difficulty functioning and had gaps in his awareness and memory. Jake felt he was visited by "entities" that deepened his confusion and estrangement and his distrust of people. He had great empathy, though, for those who were downtrodden, handicapped, or suffering from misfortunes.

In his mid-20s, he witnessed a well-dressed, wealthy woman swear and spit at a frail homeless man who had approached her for a handout. He had earlier observed the same homeless man rummaging through trashcans, looking for scraps of food or remainders of sodas. Jake became upset, followed the woman to her home, and proceeded to burglarize her house. This led to his arrest, sentencing, and incarceration. He sank further into depression and despair and regularly contemplated suicide. He acted on it soon after his discharge from prison once he secured the means.

When Jake was sent by his counselor to see me, he was still thinking about suicide and had no hope for a better future. He had no sense of his purpose in life, and he was unable to form connections with people. He thought TFT sounded like a joke. He was willing to give it a try, however, though he was skeptical about it working on his profound depression and anxiety.

As he began focusing on his symptoms of depression, Jake hesitantly started tapping on the specific acupoints we determined he needed to address, as I demonstrated on myself and tapped along with him. His facial expression gradually shifted from despair and skepticism to surprise, curiosity, hope, and excitement. Jake's SUD (subjective units of distress) rating of his depression, which was initially 10 (the most distress), dropped after each tapping sequence until he was shaking his head incredulously when he reported it was at 0 (no distress).

We then proceeded to work on the underlying issues that were now flashing back into his mind. Jake's energy level was higher. He was trembling with anxiety and fearfulness, formerly numbed by his depression. To his amazement, as he now eagerly tapped on the specific acupoints for his anxiety, his trembling ceased, and his SUD level dropped in increments from 10 down to 0.

Once his anxiety remitted, Jake spontaneously recalled the traumatic events that were probably causal. He experienced anger, rage, and guilt with the return of these memories that he had previously been apprehensive about recalling. He had spent much time and effort avoiding those still painful and vivid memories. Jake now had some confidence that he could handle these issues and diligently focused on the most disturbing memories and thoughts.

Jake's SUD rating of 20 on the 0-to-10 scale was indicative of how over-the-top these emotions were as, in the past, they had flooded him with severe panic, flashbacks, and nightmares. He had coped by numbing out in various ways and dissociating from the too-painful memories. Now as he focused on them while simultaneously decreasing his physiological arousal and distress by tapping on the specific sequence of acupoints, he could think about these traumas and experience them for the first time as distant memories. Thinking about these events no longer resulted in reliving them. Jake reported an inner sense of peace and calm that until this moment had been unknown to him.

He was astounded at the radical changes he felt physically and mentally in what seemed like mere minutes (the initial TFT session was an hour and a half). Jake was perplexed that he could feel so different. When his oppressive depression lifted and his debilitating agitation and anxiety calmed down, his whole perspective on life was transformed. His sense of tranquility and inner peace deepened over the ensuing sessions with further work on the multiple traumas in his life.

As Jake had been traumatized in his early years, he appeared to have stayed frozen and locked into his dyslexic level of functioning. He had filled out my intake forms laboriously and had large printing with numerous reversals. To both of our amazement, he appeared to move forward to integrate whatever he was currently learning, as well as to be in a calmer and more centered state, after we worked through the traumas he had endured early in life. He started journaling and writing prolifically once he no longer had posttraumatic stress symptoms, and he was able to write without reversals and with more maturity in his penmanship. This came about after several sessions, along with his diligently doing the self-treatments between sessions. Collarbone breathing (see Appendix D) was part of his protocol, and he practiced this with a treatment for psychological reversal (PR) several times a day to improve his concentration and coordination. When psychological reversal is present, it means we are in the opposite of a positive state. This can be corrected through centering ourselves by tapping on the side of the hand (the blade of the hand, also called the PR point or the Karate Chop point).

Jake began to take interest in growing things and taking care of animals. He volunteered at a food bank and helped distribute food to the homeless. He started reconnecting with family members and started socializing and getting to know more people in his community. He reached out to help others in ways that he could. He eventually developed a friendship that led to marriage, something he never envisioned in his wildest dreams.

TFT Treatments for Jake

Depression
Side of hand Gamut spot Under collarbone Index finger Middle finger Under nose Under lip Under collarbone Under eye Under collarbone 9 Gamut process Repeat acupoint sequence Reversals: tender spot, index finger, under nose
Anxiety
Side of hand Eyebrow Under eye Under arm Under collarbone Under eye Under collarbone 9 Gamut process Repeat acupoint sequence Reversals: tender spot, index finger, under nose

Trauma with Anger, Rage, and Guilt
Side of hand Eyebrow Under eye Under arm Under collarbone Tiny finger Outside edge of eye Index finger Under collarbone 9 Gamut process Repeat acupoint sequence Reversals: tender spot, index finger, under nose
Collarbone breathing (see Appendix D) for concentration and coordination preceded by psychological reversal treatment (side of hand).

3

From
Isolation to Connection

Pessimism never won any battle.

—Dwight Eisenhower

During depression, it is often intolerable for the sufferer to be around other people. Chad came to me under duress, on his doctor's referral, and only because he was opposed to taking medications regularly. Chad's physician had said he would give him a month to work on getting his blood pressure down, and if he didn't improve, he would need to start taking medication for that and also for his depression.

TFT can help with depression by reducing the physiological symptoms of increased muscular tension, rapid heartbeat, respiration changes, and looping resentful thoughts. Reducing irritability, which was another of Chad's symptoms, can facilitate better acceptance of self and others, which in turn helps to decrease the isolation and aloneness that can compound depressive feelings.

Chad described himself as antisocial because he avoided interactions with people and didn't talk to anyone unless he absolutely had to do so to survive or to keep his job. He had a technical job that allowed him to work alone, which suited him well. Even his coworkers and neighbors didn't know his full name, as he would just give his initials when asked his name. He had been a loner all his life and distrusted everyone.

In his early thirties, he started to develop high blood pressure and signs of depression. Chad had trouble sleeping, difficulty getting up in the morning, didn't enjoy watching TV, and had to force himself to eat the fast food he picked up daily. He lay around on the weekends and didn't bother to clean up his apartment other than taking out the trash. Chad reasoned that his bed and bathroom would get messed up again, so it was pointless to keep them clean. Being a loner with no friends, no one would ever see them except him anyway.

Chad felt irritable all the time. He had little tolerance for people's small talk, gossiping, and telling jokes, which he overheard whenever he worked in the proximity of other people. Yet deep down inside, he also envied their closeness and sharing with each other. He felt disconnected from the human race and only felt a bit of meaning through what he could repair with his technical skills and expertise. He grunted and acted annoyed on the rare occasions when someone bothered to thank him or comment positively on his work. Secretly though, he felt some pleasure for that brief, uncomfortable interaction.

When his doctor told him that he should start taking high blood pressure medication and antidepressants, he shook his head in protest. He didn't want to take any medication. Decades earlier, he had started drinking to numb himself from painful memories, and he had become an alcoholic. His father, who had abandoned him when Chad was 3 years old, was also an alcoholic. Chad vowed never to be like his dad. He didn't remember him that well, but his older sister told him his father was verbally, physically, and sexually abusive. Chad vaguely recalled his father swearing, yelling, and throwing a pot of stew across a room.

When Chad's drinking had taken a turn for the worse, he struggled to stop, for fear of losing his job. He started not being able to wake up to go to work and began to develop tremors in his hands. He got himself off alcohol and realized he could never have another drop again, or he would become even worse. As a result of becoming abstinent, he was averse to taking anything regularly.

Chad struggled with the intake forms, which required some personal information, and he was against having to talk to someone about himself. He told me he came only because his doctor sent him, and he did not want to talk about his personal life. He answered in gruff, monosyllabic phrases in an almost annoyed manner.

Like most people who are in tremendous pain, he was hesitant yet curious and receptive to Thought Field Therapy on the diagnostic level. This would involve energy testing to determine the treatment's meridian acupoints. Chad agreed to share a couple of words about what he was focusing on and where he was feeling it in his body. He started with his elevated blood pressure, which he felt in his heart, arms, and head. His SUD rating dropped steadily from 10 to 7 to 4 to 1 and then to 0 as he went through the various steps.

Chad immediately felt a change in his body. He stated that he felt the tension drain out. His blood pressure went from 160/90 to 140/80. He acknowledged that he had previously felt tense, irritable, angry, and he was perplexed that he felt more relaxed and didn't even feel annoyed anymore. Chad moved his neck and shoulders and expressed surprise at the looseness and increased range of motion he felt as he became more relaxed.

Encouraged by these results in his first session, he then wanted to work on his depression in the next session. Chad felt his depression was already a little different without the anger, irritability, and tension. After we worked on that, he began to have the slightest hint of a smile. He spontaneously related that he had never before felt that way, and it felt odd—like he was a stranger to himself.

Chad worked diligently on his two treatment protocols during the week before his next session. He came in wearing a shy smile instead of his usual menacing scowl. He shared that it had been a most amazing week for him as people were relating to him differently. He wasn't sure how to handle that, as, usually, no one spoke to him unless it was directly related to his job. He was surprised that several people greeted him with a "good morning," which took him aback and he didn't know how to respond. He told me that he just nodded his head and smiled. We did a little role-playing and role reversal, and when he took the role of the person initiating the greeting, he felt most gratified when he got some kind of positive response back and felt uneasy when he was ignored or got what felt like a negative response, such as the scowl he had been wearing for decades. He then practiced different positive responses to see what would feel comfortable for him and would have a positive effect on both him and the other person.

Chad then wanted to work on his distrust of people, which he felt might have come from being abandoned by his father. In the course of working on this, an early childhood trauma emerged. He recalled something that had been blocked out since he was 5 years old. He had vague recollections of being wrapped in white sheets and being held down by his mother who was holding a knife and threatening to cut off his penis. She was yelling at Chad for being a very bad boy because she had found him playing with himself. As he was working on this trauma treatment, he spontaneously hummed "Rock-a-Bye Baby" and then started crying. He recalled being told that he had been thrown into the air while his psychotic mother was singing that song to him, and he sustained injuries when he fell to the concrete floor. He was not sure how old he was then, but he knew he had been very young. Chad was removed from the home permanently after the incident with the knife.

As we continued, he spontaneously changed the notes he was humming to "Chariots of Fire" on his last round of his trauma treatment protocol. He felt a profound sense of relief and release and felt the tension, hurt, anger, and pain drain out of his body. Over the next several sessions, Chad worked on his social anxieties and development of social communication and assertion skills. He did some Gestalt work, externalizing his internal dialogues with the empty-chair role-playing to develop his communication and interaction skills, and existential therapy to establish his new meaning and purpose in life. He utilized peak performance (see Appendix E) to work on enhancing his self-confidence once he worked through his barriers to being more sociable. Chad's level of confidence went from a low of 2 to 10, the highest level attainable. His critical self-statements transformed spontaneously into positive affirmations.

Chad progressed from returning greetings to initiating greetings. He found himself wanting to tell jokes, much to his surprise and even concern, as in the past he had disdained joke telling. After practicing with role-playing, audiotaped rehearsal, self-review in front of a mirror (as he did not have access to a video camera), and peak performance repetition, Chad ventured gingerly to tell a joke to a couple of his coworkers. To his elation, they reacted with smiles and laughter and started sharing jokes with him and including him in their social conversations. To his surprise, he felt a warm feeling about being part of the group and felt "welcomed into the human race for the first time." As the weeks went by, he started initiating conversations and even greeting total strangers.

He had never been to any of his company's social events and debated going to an upcoming dinner. He became determined to go after a couple of his coworkers encouraged him to attend. He prepared for the dinner by reading the newspaper for conversation topics and learning some new jokes, as he was nervous about interacting with so many people at once. Chad role-played in session, working with TFT for his social anxiety and peak performance. He was relieved to discover that he could contribute a lot by being a good listener and found it effortless to ask relevant questions, as he truly wanted to know more about what the other person was sharing.

Chad was ecstatic about his experience at the dinner where he was popular with his coworkers. No one had ever seen him at social events, and they wanted to get to know him better. He had an opportunity to converse at least briefly with everyone he worked with and enjoyed the interchanges. Suddenly, he felt he was working with friends rather than strangers. Subsequently, different individuals or groups invited him to join them at lunch and at social or recreational events outside work.

At another company event, an enjoyable hike up a winding mountain trail, he met the sister of one of his coworkers. Chad made quite an impression on her. When he heard her exclaim that her favorite fruit was mountain apple, he created a fetching pole out of long bamboo sticks and knocked down a few for her. He heard from his coworker how impressed this delightful woman was with him, and they started dating.

Chad's sister was happy to hear that he was finally starting to go out on dates. As the relationship became serious, his sister asked if he had told the woman about what had happened to him when he was a little kid and why he couldn't have children. It was the first time they had ever discussed this. He found out that for all those years, his sister had the horrifying memories of hearing her brother screaming and seeing blood all over the white sheets. She saw her baby brother being taken away to the hospital and wasn't able to see him for years. His sister came for treatment of her secondary trauma and guilt for feeling that she should have called the police immediately and gotten neighbors sooner to help her brother. His sister was relieved to learn that their mother had not actually succeeded in mutilating Chad.

Chad beamed with joy when he came in personally to hand me an invitation to his wedding a year later. He reflected that his distrust of people had stemmed from his early life traumas, had him avoiding close interactions with people, and given him the impression that he just was not a people person. After going through a period of confusion of not knowing who and what he was anymore, he discovered, to his elation, his true sociable self.

TFT Treatments for Chad

Depression
Gamut spot Under collarbone 9 Gamut process Repeat acupoint sequence Reversals: side of hand, under nose

Trauma with Anger and Rage
Eyebrow Under eye Under arm Under collarbone Tiny finger Outside edge of eye Under collarbone 9 Gamut process Repeat acupoint sequence Reversals: side of hand, under nose

Overwhelm and Trauma with Anger, Rage, Hurt, and Guilt
Side of hand Eyebrow Under eye Under arm Under collarbone Tiny finger Outside edge of eye Middle finger Index finger Under collarbone 9 Gamut process Repeat acupoint sequence Reversals: tender spot, under nose

Anxiety with Worry
Under eye Under arm Under collarbone Under eye Under collarbone 9 Gamut process Repeat acupoint sequence Reversals: side of hand, tender spot, under nose

Anger, Rage, Hurt, Trauma with Obsessive Thoughts
Tiny finger Outside edge of eye Middle finger Eyebrow Under eye Under arm Under collarbone Under eye Under collarbone 9 Gamut process Repeat acupoint sequence

FEAR/PANIC

4

Unpeeling the Layers

An optimist sees an opportunity in every calamity, a pessimist sees a calamity in every opportunity.

—Winston Churchill

When fear becomes an everyday, chronic condition, a cascade of consequences such as sleep disturbances, gastrointestinal upset, increased vigilance and worry, and mental fatigue from being on red alert around the clock can occur. These physiological manifestations can ultimately lead to functional impairment—limiting potential and ending in depression. Some people have generalized anxiety, living with worry about all sorts of things. Others have more specific anxiety disorders, such as a fear of heights or specific phobias.

Geo would not ride in elevators even to attend a mandatory work meeting on the 40th floor. He would climb the stairs, out of breath and struggling from the exertion, while not letting anyone know he was terrified about being confined in an elevator. After all, he was a combat veteran and a leader in his workplace. How could he let people know about such a stupid fear when he had experienced war? Geo had learned to hide his phobia and did so quite well for many years.

Hesitantly, he came to see me, stating that he didn't want to "talk about feelings or that kind of stuff" but was interested in TFT. He had heard about amazing results from friends and colleagues who had encouraged him to check it out. After sharing a brief history with me and getting an explanation of TFT, he agreed that the best way to learn about it was by actually doing it.

He thought it all sounded hokey and silly but less onerous to him than traditional talk therapy where he'd have to focus on feelings and emotions. Geo started with a SUD level of 10, and began tapping on the demonstrated acupoints and continuing through the serial steps of the protocol for phobias. He was pleasantly surprised to find his fear of elevators going down to 8, then 6, then 4. He was just beginning to feel that he could get into an elevator again when he suddenly recalled the time when he crash-landed in a helicopter. He described the door being jammed shut and how he and his crewmates desperately tried to get out before anything ignited or exploded.

We shifted to the now more prominent trauma, which was at a SUD level of 10. Beads of perspiration appeared on his forehead as he recalled those terrifying minutes of being trapped. Those several minutes felt like an eternity as they all fought against time to break out of the potential incinerator, using every ounce of strength to escape. He relived those desperate moments, feeling his heart race and adrenaline pump through his veins. Eventually, he began to calm down as his SUD rating dropped to 7, then to 4. Tears streamed down his face, and his body heaved with sobs as the mental image in his thought field morphed into his horror at seeing the coffin close on his beloved father who died suddenly of a heart attack when Geo was 2 years old.

He started to recall what had been blocked from his conscious memory for four decades. Geo remembered trying to wake his father, desperately reaching out to touch him while his grieving grandparents pulled him away. He was bewildered but determined to awaken his dad. He screamed at everyone for not letting him help his father get up. He became even more furious when he saw the coffin being closed on his sleeping father. His SUD level was 10 plus, and he was shaking with rage and terror. Geo started tapping on this thought field, and his overwhelming emotions dropped from 10 plus to 6 to 4, then down to 1, then to 0.

He instantly had insight into his fear of small confined spaces. He had long suspected that his elevator phobia was connected to the downed-helicopter experience but had no inkling of its earlier related trauma when he was 2 years old and did not understand that his father had died. When he thought of the jammed door in the helicopter, his SUD was now 0, and he was grateful for them all making it out safely.

When we refocused on his fear of elevators, he threw his head back and laughed heartily. He exclaimed that his fear was gone and he thought it was ridiculous for him to have been so afraid and avoidant all these years.

We tested it out by going to a nearby high-rise building with an elevator. He rode up and down by himself without any qualms. He found it hard to fathom his previous fear and avoidance.

Geo was fascinated at his transformation and later took the TFT Algorithm Training so he could help others who had similar fears and traumas. He still marvels at how he worked through the "lump-shoe-tooth" layers of his fears.

Dr. Roger Callahan uses a tooth-shoe-lump analogy of layered problems becoming unveiled as each layer is worked through, like peeling an onion. A man with a severe toothache goes to his dentist to get care, and the pain in his jaw is all he can think about as he's sitting in the dentist's office, waiting his turn. He finally gets into the dentist's chair, his toothache is treated, and his pain is relieved. As he goes back out to the reception area, he notices his left foot hurts as he walks. He stops to take his shoe off and finds a pebble in his shoe. Now as he sits down in the same spot in the waiting room, a lump in the couch that he's sitting on bothers him, and he then notices that there is a broken spring in the couch. Many people present with the problem that has the highest level of pain or distress. Once that is resolved, they then become more aware of lesser-level pain or distress. The reverse can also be true, as in Geo's case, where he first focused on the lump, got to the shoe, and finally got to the tooth.

TFT Treatments for Geo

Phobia
Under eye Under arm Under collarbone 9 Gamut process Repeat acupoint sequence Reversals: side of hand, under nose

Trauma
Eyebrow Under eye Under arm Under collarbone 9 Gamut process Repeat acupoint sequence Reversals: side of hand, under nose

Trauma with Rage
Eyebrow Under eye Under arm Under collarbone Outside edge of eye Under collarbone 9 Gamut process Repeat acupoint sequence Reversals: side of hand, tender spot, under nose

5

From Panic to Purpose

You may have to fight a battle more than once to win it.

—Margaret Thatcher

I see many clients who suffer from debilitating panic attacks. Symptoms can include a racing heart, shortness of breath, lightheadedness, thinking the worst, wobbly legs, shaking, and extreme distress. Some were so frightened that they began avoiding situations in which they experienced the panic attack. As the contexts for the panics broadened with subsequent panic episodes, their spheres of avoidance increased, and their operating worlds shrank significantly. The ultimate confinement is agoraphobia—fear and anxiety about venturing out anywhere.

Fortunately, TFT has been an ideal empowerment tool for people to reclaim their lives and re-expand their world, as it is a self-administered treatment that can be utilized anywhere, anytime, and can be done mentally if needed. One of my colleagues, a psychiatric nurse, used to dread seeing clients with panic disorder until he learned TFT. Since using TFT, clients with panic disorder have become his favorite disorder to treat!

I recall a particular client who was finding it increasingly difficult to function in his work, family relationships, and social life. Manuel's attacks included shortness of breath, heart palpitations, shakiness, dizziness, queasy stomach, and racing thoughts of dire consequences. He was so preoccupied with the possibility of an attack that he started avoiding all situations and places where he had experienced one. He felt that the walls of his life were closing in on him and confining him to an increasingly limited existence. He was a prisoner of his panic attacks. They prevented him from going on trips and out to public events, restaurants, movies, and grocery stores. Manuel questioned whether living this way was worth it, and he felt guilty about being so dependent on others, as he could not do much for himself and he was unable to contribute to the enjoyment of others. He slipped further and further into depressive feelings, taking no pleasure in life and having no energy to do anything.

Initially, he had positive responses to antidepressants and antianxiety medications, with improvement in his sleep patterns and appetite. Over time, he had less response to the medications, even after increases in dosages and changes to alternative medications. After 3 years, he wondered whether they were helping at all. He had not attained remission of his panic attacks, had no reversal of his avoidance behaviors, and had no lessening of his basic depression. Agitation and despair both increased tremendously. He began having suicidal thoughts, and developed a tremor, which made certain activities even more challenging and frustrating.

His psychiatrist referred him to me to try different approaches. I noticed right away how Manuel had bitten his fingernails down to the quick and nervously pulled at his hair. I could see how anxiety had manifested in his life. Manuel responded well to TFT treatment of his panic attacks and felt his palpitations fade. His breath calmed into a slower and deeper rhythm, and his catastrophic thoughts vanished as he tapped. To his amazement, he found that he could mitigate a panic attack in progress within a few rounds of the panic protocol.

Manuel found through the pulse test (see Appendix F) and individualized energy sensitivities TFT diagnostic protocol that he was sensitive to wheat, MSG, and pesticide sprays. By avoiding these substances, he reduced his panic attack triggers. He had been aware that his voice got raspy after eating his daily sandwiches, but he had not associated this with his panic episodes, which occurred often more than an hour after his meal. Through doing regular TFT treatments and avoiding wheat, MSG, and the other substances, his panic episodes diminished in frequency as well as intensity until, after about 2 months, he no longer experienced them.

With the resolution of his panic attacks, Manuel felt more in control again. He felt a significant change in his perspective on life and began to participate in other therapies to help his depression. Existential therapy helped Manuel define a deeper sense of what made his heart sing. Cognitive behavioral therapy guided him in challenging his negative beliefs and attitudes and helped him reframe his perspective on life. Although he had been introduced to these therapies before, he reported that he was not able to benefit fully from them because he had difficulty sustaining the focus, concentration, and mental shifting required. It wasn't until TFT calmed his agitation and elevated his energy level that he had the ability to focus and concentrate.

TFT treatment also addressed his depression and he found that his mood and energy level increased gradually. He began to look forward to activities he could participate in again. Reciprocal inhibition and response prevention augmented by TFT helped him gain control over his compulsive nail-biting and hair-pulling, which increased his sense of self-control and confidence as well as his self-esteem.

He felt joy in life again, started enjoying activities with his wife and family, and initiated outings and surprises. He wanted to give back to the community and volunteered his services at nursing and senior homes. Manuel felt better than he had ever felt before, with positive energy, stable moods, greater satisfaction, and with clarity of purpose and meaning in his life.

TFT Treatments for Manuel

Panic
Eyebrow Under eye Under arm Under collarbone 9 Gamut process Repeat acupoint sequence Reversals: side of hand, tender spot, index finger, under nose

Depression with Recurrent Negative Thinking
Gamut spot Under collarbone Under eye Under collarbone 9 Gamut process Repeat acupoint sequence Reversals: side of hand, tender spot, index finger, under nose

Low Self-Esteem
Side of hand Index finger Eyebrow Under eye Under arm Under collarbone Under eye Under collarbone Under nose Under lip 9 Gamut process Repeat acupoint sequence Reversals: tender spot, index finger, under nose

Urge to Bite Fingernails
Side of hand Tiny finger Outside edge of eye Middle finger Index finger Under collarbone Under eye Under collarbone 9 Gamut process Repeat acupoint sequence Reversals: tender spot, index finger, under nose
Urge to Pull Hair
Side of hand Index finger Middle finger Tiny finger Eyebrow Under collarbone Under eye Under collarbone 9 Gamut process Repeat acupoint sequence Reversals: tender spot, index finger, under nose
Note: If symptoms recur, Dr. Arthur Coca's pulse test (see Appendix F) and log of what you eat, drink, or inhale is one way to collect information that can help identify triggering energy sensitivities. Manuel found through the pulse test and intake-and-exposure log that wheat, foods with MSG, and pesticide sprays appeared to contribute to triggering his panic symptoms, and he was able to confirm this through systematic elimination of each in turn.

6

From Panic to Peace

Optimism is the faith that leads to achievement. Nothing can be done without hope and confidence.

—Helen Keller

Jasper, a successful business executive, began to experience frequent panic attacks in his mid-30s. He never had them at work, although he had stressful moments at his demanding job. He reported neither overwhelming work pressures nor marital distress (he was married with no children). His attacks occurred almost daily, either during the night or first thing in the morning. He would awaken sweating, heart pounding, struggling to breathe. He had tried medications but didn't like the dulled feeling that accompanied them.

He wanted something that could help him but not affect his performance or mental state. Jasper came in to try Energy Psychology after he had heard a colleague tell him how helpful TFT had been in eliminating his posttraumatic stress disorder symptoms.

Jasper was astounded to find that merely tapping on the acupoints on the eyebrow, under eye, under arm, and under his collarbone allowed him to attain a deeper sense of relaxation than he had ever been able to achieve with his hour-long meditations. While the breathing meditations had been very helpful in notably reducing the tension in his body and mind, they did not get rid of his panic attacks. Jasper started diligently practicing all the components of his TFT panic treatment. He could diminish the panic symptoms rapidly when he felt them, but he wondered what caused the panic attacks in the first place and was willing to do the detective work to find out.

Using Dr. Arthur Coca's pulse test and log (see Appendix F), he confirmed what he had known from his years of experience with his panic attacks. They happened during the night (his pulse would rise into the 90s) and in the mornings. But during the day, his pulse generally ranged in the 70s. Since the timing and location of his elevated pulse rates were at home, he wondered, half-jokingly, if he might be allergic to his wife. The TFT diagnostic level was used to test the things Jasper suspected from his pulse log might be contributory, and a systematic process of elimination then tested the various things in his bedroom to which his body indicated having some sensitivity. Using the TFT diagnostic energy testing, this included the bedding. After the bedding had been washed, his pulse reading was lower.

Jasper then thoughtfully speculated that it might be his three cats that had free reign in and out of his bedroom. He often played with them before he retired to bed. Jasper decided to test his hypothesis. He had all the bedding washed again and had the carpets and drapes vacuumed, but, this time, he kept his beloved cats out of the bedroom. To his surprise, he woke up with no panic attacks and with a pulse of 65. He was elated at finding the trigger for his panic attacks, although he was saddened and disappointed to find out it was related to some of the greatest joys of his home life.

He subsequently realized that the few times that he had had panic attacks while driving to work were when he had a lighter schedule, so he had more time to frolic with his cats before going to work. He now understood why he had those attacks while in the car.

Jasper related that, fortunately, he had made the discovery himself through use of the pulse log. His cats were such an important part of his life that had I suggested he try keeping his cats out of his bedroom, he would have been so upset that he would not have rationally problem-solved how to keep his cats in the house and at the same time avoid triggering his panic symptoms.

Subsequently, Jasper treated one of his cats and helped a neighbor's cat with TFT, which can be administered to animals when they are experiencing a state needing to be treated. Both cats had been traumatized by an aggressive dog that had gotten loose in the neighborhood, so they could be treated when they displayed fearfulness when dogs were in proximity to them.

Jasper felt more energy with the remission of his panic attacks. He felt peace and gratitude for his great life, and this led him to volunteer to feed the homeless on holidays, and to contribute to fund-raising for humanitarian efforts.

TFT Treatments for Jasper

Panic
Eyebrow Under eye Under arm Under collarbone 9 Gamut process Repeat acupoint sequence Reversals: side of hand, tender spot, index finger, under nose Pulse test and log (see Appendix F)

7
Flying Free

It is better to light a candle than curse the darkness.

—-Eleanor Roosevelt

TFT is very effective as a treatment for phobias. A phobia I encounter a lot in my practice is fear of flying. Obviously, this can limit mobility and full enjoyment of life. I have worked successfully with many phobias. In the rare situation of a phobia being the only problem, it can sometimes be resolved in only one session of learning the TFT phobia protocol.

One example is Devin and Dolly, a couple in their middle 60s who both had a phobia of flying. Neither had traveled off the island where they were born and lived because of their fear of flying. After retiring from fulfilling careers, they were increasingly envious of their friends who were traveling all over the world and regaling them with stories and videos of their exciting adventures. They also longed to see historic sites, experience the grandeur of natural wonders like the Grand Canyon, participate in international events like the Olympics, and visit the homelands where their grandparents grew up. They had always rationalized that traveling would be the same as watching travel videos from the comfort of their couch. But now Dolly and Devin felt that they were missing out on what could be an exciting and gratifying expansion of this new phase of their lives.

After one session of working with the standard phobia protocol, they felt brave enough to try a short flight to a neighboring island. They drove down to the airport to purchase their tickets so they could sit in the parking lot and tap through their phobia protocols and peak performance (see Appendix E) as they watched the planes take off and land. They envisioned themselves being on those planes.

After they felt comfortable when thinking about flying, they took a 30-minute flight from Oahu to Maui. After this successful flight, they then took a longer flight to Hawaii, and then they ventured to the West Coast and visited California.

After that gratifying and rewarding trip, including fun excursions to Universal Studios, Disneyland, and other sites, they were eager for more and started traveling every 4 months to the places they had long dreamed of experiencing. They were so full of gratitude for their abundant lives and adventures that they wanted to help others be able to travel too. They reached out to people who were landlocked by their fears, shared their story, and invited them to explore the world with them, teaching acquaintances as well as strangers how to be free of fear of flying. Dolly and Devin also joined friends in new adventures and sometimes included newly unstuck traveling enthusiasts.

TFT Treatments for Dolly and Devin

Phobia
Under eye Under arm Under collarbone 9 Gamut process Repeat acupoint sequence Reversals: side of hand, tender spot, index finger, under nose

STRESS/ANXIETY

8

A Victim No More

Most folks are about as happy as they make up their minds to be.
—Abraham Lincoln

In the past few years, bullying has captured national attention, as we've seen horrible video footage of young people being victimized in terrible ways. Social media, a virtual necessity in teen life, is sometimes used as a weapon to harass and single out someone who doesn't fit in. Any parent of a child who has suffered at the hands of bullies knows the devastating repercussions. Bullying isn't a recent phenomenon, but the violence involved has certainly escalated. Aside from the physical effects of being bullied, the mental and emotional traumas can last throughout a person's life, sadly affecting their adult existence.

I've treated many adults for severe anxiety resulting from childhood bullying. When people are bullied, they are subjected to traumatizing events repeatedly, and their self-esteem and self-confidence suffer. Children are often powerless and have not yet developed the skills to defend themselves. One such child was Annette, an 11-year-old girl who was brought to me by her mother because she'd become a victim of relentless bullies at her school.

Annette cried and was anxious every school day. She daily resisted going to school and often had nightmares about being teased, pushed around, and harassed by her classmates. Her public elementary school had a "no tolerance for bullying" policy, but the kids found ways around this. Her concerned mother had several conferences with Annette's teachers and school administrators, who then intervened with lectures, sanctions, and tolerance trainings. The harassment went underground, however, with snide remarks, gestures, menacing scowls, glares, and other lower profile, intimidating behaviors that went under teachers' radar.

Her mother could not afford to send Annette to a private school, as she was struggling to manage basic rent and food expenses on her modest salary as a custodial worker. She brought Annette in to see me on the recommendation of the school counselor. Annette was initially anxious about recounting what she had endured at school but was eager to learn some skills that would help her with her fears and nightmares.

In her first session, we started with Annette tapping on the side of her hand to get grounded and centered, and to diminish her self-doubt. She rated her stress level at over 10, as she could not conceive of how she could function at school as long as the bullies were there. This centering tapping point was helpful in her feeling that she was taking control into, literally, her own hands. We then worked through her frightening memories and flashbacks of being pushed around and threatened by several children. Annette whispered in a raspy, quivering voice her fear of being seriously hurt or killed by the bullies, as they had once threatened her. She exhibited much trepidation, her voice trembling, her eyes wide with fear, holding her breath or breathing erratically, and her extremities shaking. She appeared on the verge of tears, and she related that her heart was racing. As she tapped on the acupoints, she was quite surprised to find her racing heart calm down and her shaking cease. Annette heaved a deep sigh of relief and found herself actually breathing normally as she continued her tapping sequences.

As she peeled away the layers of fearful experiences, her face broke out into a broad grin, and she felt she could be strong and follow strategies to be safer, such as not going alone into campus areas where she could be harassed. In subsequently working on peak performance (see Appendix E) and imagining herself navigating on campus, she grinned even more broadly as she said she was braver than the bullies. She explained that as she visualized walking with a friend into the bathroom where the bullies gathered together often, she realized that they must be very insecure since they had to go around in packs and picked on children who were alone.

Annette could see that the bullies were intimidating her by threatening to hurt and kill her because they were fearful of getting into trouble with the school authorities and perhaps their parents if she reported what they were doing. She laughed aloud as she spontaneously visualized what they were feeling on the inside and even thought they might be bullying her and others because they themselves might be picked on at home by harsh parents. Annette's ability to "get inside the head" of her bullies showed remarkable maturity and healing. She wondered if some might be jealous of her close relationship with her mother. She was aware that some of their parents never attended parent nights or meetings with teachers while her caring mother came to every school event and volunteered to help with class excursions.

In the course of seven sessions, Annette's trauma and anxieties diminished to a SUD level of 0 with her TFT treatments. But while her anxiety became less and less, some mild reactive depression surfaced. She responded rapidly to TFT for depression over the following three sessions. She was then able to access her hurt and anger, which she generally had suppressed and turned inward. Annette's posture straightened, and she sat and stood taller after working through her hurt and anger with the TFT algorithm. She exclaimed with a wide grin and firm conviction that she was not feeling so scared anymore.

We then worked with peak performance, and she visualized with all her sensory modalities how she'd handle encounters in the classroom, in the cafeteria, and on the playground. Annette's confidence level rose from a rating of 0 to 5 after TFT for her trauma, anxiety, depression, hurt, and anger. After doing peak performance, she jumped up from her chair to give me a high five. With tears welling up in her eyes, she exclaimed triumphantly that her confidence level had gone all the way up to 10!

We practiced doing all her treatments mentally without physically tapping the acupoints so that she could discretely use the appropriate TFT treatment anywhere and anytime she needed them. Annette related, after having successful experiences at school, that she was beginning to make friends with many of her classmates, including a couple of children who had previously joined in with the bullies. She started to look forward to school. Her mother beamed with pride as she observed how Annette was blossoming academically and socially. Annette described herself as "a happy camper," no longer intimidated by the world around her but learning how to navigate successfully and skillfully through any hazards she came across. She noted that she could think much more clearly and "make smart choices and decisions" when she was not flooded with fear that made her "brain freeze up."

A few months after her TFT treatments, she helped a fellow student who was being picked on by the bullies. She shared her own experience and understanding with her classmate and showed her how to do the treatments for trauma and anger. She was ecstatic that her new friend started feeling more courageous and started standing up for herself. Annette declared that she wanted to study diligently so that she could go to college and become a social worker or psychologist to help children who were suffering from fears and anxieties that held them back from their studies or socialization.

The consequences of bullying—which are fear and intimidation; impaired concentration, learning, and functioning; low self-esteem; chronic anxiety; and depression and suicidal tendencies—are immeasurable costs for the victim as well as the bully who may be acting out his/her own prior traumas. TFT and Energy Psychology methods would be empowering and healing additions to the toolbox of every counselor and educator.

TFT Treatments for Annette

Grounding and Centering
Side of hand

Trauma
Eyebrow Under eye Under arm Under collarbone 9 Gamut process Repeat acupoint sequence Side of hand

Trauma with Anger, Shame, and Embarrassment
Side of hand Eyebrow Under eye Under arm Under collarbone Tiny finger Under collarbone Under nose Under lip 9 Gamut process Repeat acupoint sequence Reversal: under nose

Trauma with Anger and Rage
Side of hand Eyebrow Under eye Under arm Under collarbone Tiny finger Outside edge of eye Under collarbone 9 Gamut process Repeat acupoint sequence

Trauma with Hurt and Depression
Eyebrow Under eye Under arm Under collarbone Middle finger Tiny finger Gamut spot Under collarbone Reversal: side of hand
Peak performance for coping with the bullies (see Appendix E).

9

From Work Stress to Satisfaction

Be faithful in small things because it is in them that your strength lies.
—Mother Teresa

Workplace stress has increased dramatically in the last 20 years. With the downsizing of resources, proliferation of needed knowledge, ever-changing and improving advances in technology, and increased workplace demands, there is no longer a clear distinction between work and home. In many workplaces, people are expected to accomplish greater volumes of work and higher complexities of tasks than they had previously.

Hugo found himself increasingly stressed as work demands increased relentlessly. As he tended to be somewhat of a perfectionist, he had always struggled with getting his work completed on time. He worked extra hours to ensure that everything was done correctly for the construction firm where he had worked for 10 years. As upgrades were made in the computer programs and interfaces, his stress level began to rise as he learned the new information, integrating it with the old information while still trying to keep up with his work output.

His already limited physical activity of walking or swimming once a week dropped to once a month and then to none. He began to eat more and more fast food. While Hugo had some occasional fruit, his main sustenance was drive-through hamburgers and fries with diet sodas and chocolate sundaes. His work hours stretched from 9 to 14 hours and from 5.5 days to 7 days a week.

Hugo started experiencing chest tightness and tension in his neck, arms, and shoulders, and he went to see his medical doctor, who examined and tested him thoroughly. His doctor found that Hugo had mild hypertension, high blood sugar, and high cholesterol in sharp contrast to his within-normal-range scores across the board just a few years prior. His doctor recommended medications. Hugo resisted but agreed to seek counseling for his stress.

After relating his history and current situation, Hugo was eager to try TFT. He responded well to a combination of stress/anxiety plus obsessiveness protocols. He went from a SUD rating of 10 down to 0 and felt the tightness in his body disappear. To his surprise, his compelled sense of having to do things perfectly lightened up. He continued the protocol at least three to four times a day and found his obsessiveness continued to lessen further every day. He was then able to begin exercising 15 to 30 minutes daily, going to 45 to 60 minutes on the weekends. Hugo also started practicing healthier eating habits, which included more vegetables, a lot less meat, reduced carbohydrates, and eliminating desserts. He found his sleep lengthened and deepened, his energy rebounded, and his concentration was better sustained. He used collarbone breathing (see Appendix D) to improve his focus, attention, and concentration. Hugo was actually more productive in less time and was able to get his work done in 5 days a week, 8 to 9 hours a day. His blood pressure, blood sugar, and cholesterol levels were back within normal range when he had his return medical visit.

Hugo was grateful for the increased time and energy he had, and now he had the time and motivation to help others enjoy their lives more. He volunteered to help with youth sports activities at his church and got even more exercise as well as greater joy and satisfaction in his life.

TFT Treatments for Hugo

Stress/Anxiety plus Obsessiveness
Side of hand

Trauma
Under eye Under arm Under collarbone Under eye Under collarbone 9 Gamut process Repeat acupoint sequence Reversals: side of hand, tender spot, under nose

Collarbone breathing (see Appendix D) for concentration.

ANGER/RAGE

10

From Felon to Role Model

You cannot shake hands with a clenched fist.

—Indira Gandhi, former prime minister of India

Anger is such a huge topic that a whole book could be written on it. I have chosen a few cases that have stood out to me over the years. These cases show remarkable healing and bravery on the part of the clients involved. Whether people come in for depression, anxiety, abuse, stress, or whatever ails them, anger or rage nearly always rears its head in treatments.

We all deal with frustrations and anger in our daily lives. What sets these cases apart is how anger can imprison us and hold us back from living a fulfilling, happy life. Anger is but a symptom of deeper underlying hurt. It is a defensive weapon used to keep more pain out and is used to hurt others or the self as a misguided way of treating the pain. What can make treatment so tricky is that anger often feels so self-justified that the client cannot see past his or her hurt. Yet it's necessary to do so in order for healing to begin.

Bud's vocational rehabilitation counselor referred him to me. He had been in prison more than he'd been out of prison in his young adult life. He erupted into rages, often set off when he felt affronted about his race. He had been through counseling during his incarcerations in juvenile detention as well as with his parole officers and had completed two different anger management treatment programs. He wistfully told me he did think about the consequences of his actions—usually after the fact when he was already sitting in jail. He came from a family of "rageahol-ics" and assumed it was some kind of hereditary bad-temper curse that ran in his family. His family history was rife with alcoholism and violence, and Bud drank a lot too. He sobered up each time he was incarcerated, but it never lasted after he got out. He had challenges completing any program that involved other people since he had a low tolerance for frus-tration and often got into blowups that ended with him doing damage to people or property or both.

Initially, he laughed scornfully when I talked to him about TFT. He thought it sounded crazy that he might be able to control his profound rage and hair-trigger temper by tapping on himself. He muttered that it would take much more than tapping on himself to tame the extreme rages he had experienced throughout his life. He began to consider it, however, when I explained that it would either help or do nothing, and there were no negative side effects reported in 40 years of use. I also shared situations of other people recovering from their own violent rages. Bud then decided it would not hurt to try it, though he was still sure it would not do anything for his intense level of rage.

After learning about how TFT is done, he focused on his anger and related trauma, which brought his SUD level to a 15 on the 0–10 scale. He followed my demonstration of the treatment steps on myself as he tapped himself on the modeled acupoints. As he started tapping on the acupoints for this treatment of anger, rage, and trauma, Bud's round eyes widened even farther. He was astonished to find himself uncoiling from his tensed state despite his skepticism, and as his arms, shoulders, neck, and back relaxed, he felt his heart calm, which in turn deepened his relaxation. Bud discovered that when he was calm, he could actually think more clearly and objectively and access the tools to help him man-age his thoughts and emotions.

At his next session, Bud grinned from ear to ear. He explained that TFT worked but in a different way, and it had kept him out of trouble with the law. He told me what happened. At the gym, Bud had been provoked by a young man who made some challenging remarks. Usually, he would immediately see red and react like a raging bull whose fight-mode button had been pressed. Bud started by vigorously tapping on the Karate Chop point on his hand (side of hand) to get himself grounded and centered and told the challenger to back off. The challenger, not as muscular as Bud, was taken aback by Bud's tapping actions and yelled out, "You're crazy, man!" He backed up and ran away. Bud chuckled as he realized that TFT could work in more ways than one to keep him out of jail. He continued tapping on the rest of the anger and rage treatment as he realized he did not have to go after the challenge and fight the guy, as he would have in the not-too-distant past.

A few weeks later, another incident occurred that truly showed Bud that the treatment worked and his anger was under control. He had been minding his own business at the park when a man approached him and began harassing him. It was exactly the kind of challenging confrontation that had led to repeated violent episodes and arrests in the state where he used to live. Bud immediately began tapping on his Karate Chop point as he told the harasser, who was swearing at him and using racial slurs, that he did not want to hurt him and to leave him alone.

The burly guy continued harassing him and then started to try and punch Bud. This would normally have touched off an explosive fury from him that would not have ended well. His blind fury would have prevented him from making any type of rational decision. But Bud kept doing his TFT protocol and continued to tap physically on the treatment acupoints. We had discussed doing the treatments mentally, but when he became threatened, he couldn't do them mentally. He continued to warn the guy to back off, but the man continued to egg him on, taunting him and throwing blows that Bud mostly dodged as he continued tapping.

A small crowd had gathered around them by this time, and someone had called the police. Bud saw four officers coming toward them, and his first thought was that he would be arrested yet again. The officers pulled Bud and his challenger away from each other. To Bud's surprise, the people in the crowd explained to the police officers that the challenger was harassing Bud, using racial slurs and throwing punches at him. They explained that Bud was just hitting himself and telling the challenger to back off and leave him alone. Bud tried to explain that he was not hitting himself but was doing Thought Field Therapy to control his anger. Another officer apparently had checked on the identification of Bud and his challenger, and the officer complimented Bud on his self-control. He then shook Bud's hand! Bud almost didn't believe what had just happened. He beamed with pride as he related this incident to me.

After that event and with focused interpersonal therapy, his perspective broadened, and he was able to experience empathy for others for the first time. He began to feel emotions that were foreign due to the fact that he had suppressed everything except rage his whole life. He experienced initial confusion about who he was and what he was really all about. As sessions progressed, his range of emotions and thoughts broadened in ways that boggled his mind. He had to work his way through his maze of confusion about his lifelong beliefs about the world and himself, and the empathy that he now felt for others, especially those who had been the victims of his rage, anger, and resentment in the past. He could feel their fear, pain, and survival rage and could understand their defensive reactions and could even wonder about their own troubled and quite possibly traumatic backgrounds.

Bud was able to learn a trade and get a stable job that enabled him to support himself adequately because his training programs and apprenticeships were not being disrupted by arrests and incarcerations. He found that he could communicate positively with coworkers and started to socialize more with others. Bud worked on his episodic alcohol abuse with TFT and could lessen his cravings and control his habit. He was able to attend AA meetings and not get into fights. He found that he could now benefit from the support of his AA group, and he connected with a helpful sponsor. Bud used the TFT addiction protocol faithfully and regularly.

As Bud put it, he could not go back down that old rage road again now that he had feelings. He worked on how he could make restitution to those he had hurt in the past through acts of service in the community. He wanted to return to his home state to see how he could help with wayward, rage-filled youth to contribute to efforts to steer them away from a life of drugs and violence toward a more meaningful life. He expressed regret that his mother had passed away before she could see his change from an angry, troubled felon to a calmer, stable man with a steady job and a new sense of purpose.

TFT Treatments for Bud

Grounding and Centering
Side of hand
Rage and Anger
Outside edge of eye Tiny finger Under collarbone 9 Gamut process Repeat acupoint sequence Reversals: side of hand, tender spot, under nose
Trauma with Rage
Eyebrow Under eye Under arm Under collarbone Outside edge of eye Under collarbone 9 Gamut process Repeat acupoint sequence Reversals: side of hand, under nose

Trauma with Guilt
Eyebrow Under eye Under arm Under collarbone Index finger Under collarbone 9 Gamut process Repeat acupoint sequence Reversals: side of hand, under nose
Peak performance (see Appendix E) for controlling his rage under harassment.

11

From Avenging Rage to Promoting Prevention

The ultimate measure of a man is not where he stands in moments of comfort and convenience, but where he stands at times of challenge and controversy.

—Martin Luther King Jr.

As I mentioned in the previous chapter, self-justified anger is often the hardest to overcome. People who suffer from the difficult blows of life believe they have a right to act out on their anger even if it's harmful to others. For example, when a parent loses a child, it is one of the most challenging situations anyone could face. I have worked with many survivors of genocide and, thus, many parents who have lost their children.

Bruce was totally devastated by the murder of his oldest son from whom he had been inseparable for many years. They shared the same passion for football, hunting, and skiing, and could spend hours messing around with each other or silently sharing a priceless moment. After his son's death, Bruce felt life would never be the same and he could not see going on without him. He shook with rage as he thought of the man who snuffed out his son's life and vowed to avenge his son's death. When Bruce found out that his son's murderer would be getting out of prison, he started planning his revenge.

He became totally consumed by his rage. He incessantly ranted on about the unfairness of life and how he "needed to make things right." He spoke under his breath, repeating how he would see that justice was done. Bruce had been drinking himself to sleep nightly in futile attempts to numb the painful and haunting memories of finding his son's body. Those terrifying images were as vivid and heart wrenching as they had been years before when he came across an apparent murder victim and then realized, to his horror, that it was his own son. His profound grief weighed on him so heavily that he could not be there for his wife and surviving children who not only lost their beloved son and brother, but simultaneously lost their active, caring husband and father.

For safety and other considerations, Bruce had been sent thousands of miles away to an alcohol and drug treatment program so he would not be in the vicinity when his son's murderer walked out of prison. He obsessed about killing the murderer and subsequently killing himself to end his misery. He monopolized group time with his ranting and talked of nothing else in individual sessions. Though substance abuse is usually dealt with and stabilized first, his substance abuse counselors asked me to see him for psychotherapy to deal with his rage.

My first impression of Bruce was that he was obviously enraged, hostile, and angry at the world. With his clenched fists and rigid jaw, it became immediately apparent how worked up he was. I wondered what kind of toll the anger was taking on his body. His voice boomed with hostility, and he voiced displeasure at being sent away as if he were the criminal.

As he shared what it was like to find his son, I empathized as a parent with how incredibly traumatizing and painful it must have been. He went on to tell me how he tried to block it out with drinking, but it hadn't really worked as the flashbacks and nightmares were as vivid and horrifying as ever. Pastors, counselors, friends, and family had tried to console him, shift his thoughts, and ease his painful memories, to no avail. Medications only made him groggy and actually increased his thoughts of suicide.

Bruce indicated that he wanted the flashbacks and nightmares to dim. He realized they stirred him up and kept his anger at a constantly high level. They also led to him obsessing about avenging his son's murder and ending his own suffering and loss. He was open to trying something different, although he protested when he heard the brief explanation about TFT. He just could not see how something like that would help with his unbearable pain.

He followed my lead on doing the TFT treatment for his trauma and rage. His eyes opened wide in amazement as his shoulders began to relax and his neck appeared to elongate. His shoulders and jaw immediately loosened, and his voice became lighter. Bruce stated with incredulousness that his SUD level went from 20 (on a 0-to-10 scale) to an 8. We continued through the subsequent steps to reduce his trauma and rage further, and he went to a 5, then 3, then 1, then 0. He looked like a different person, and his perspectives started to shift. Bruce began talking about the needs of his wife and other children.

In subsequent sessions, it became apparent that Bruce had a lot of guilt about his son. He was upset for not recognizing that his son was getting involved in drugs. He had ignored the warning signs that, in hindsight, he realized were there. He made a vow to see that his son had not died in vain by dedicating time to help other teenagers become aware of the dark realities of drug abuse and dependence and what could be done to break free safely.

He has deep conversations now with his other children and hopes that they can talk freely to him about the challenges they face. Bruce has spoken to many teens and shared his story to help many youths avoid what his son experienced. He has found a new meaning and purpose in his life again in helping others to avoid the same tragedy his son and family endured.

TFT Treatments for Bruce

Trauma with Rage
Eyebrow Under eye Under arm Under collarbone Outside edge of eye Under collarbone 9 Gamut process Repeat acupoint sequence Reversals: side of hand, under nose

Trauma with Guilt
Eyebrow Under eye Under arm Under collarbone Index finger Under collarbone 9 Gamut process Repeat acupoint sequence Reversals: side of hand, tender spot, under nose

Overwhelming Grief/Depression
Side of hand Gamut spot Under collarbone 9 Gamut process Repeat acupoint sequence Reversals: tender spot, index finger, under nose

Addictive Urges
Under eye Under arm Under collarbone 9 Gamut process Repeat acupoint sequence Reversals: side of hand, tender spot, index finger, under nose

12

A Family Heals

Failure is only the opportunity to begin again more intelligently.

—Henry Ford

Though I most often treat individual clients, I am sometimes fortunate to treat an entire family. To see TFT make a big difference in families' lives is one of the most rewarding aspects of my job. Nothing can tear a family apart like out-of-control anger. I've witnessed how devastating actions and harsh words can deeply wound people.

Children who grow up with hostility and rage often repeat the pattern themselves despite vowing to never be like their parents. Developing healthier relational and communication patterns is more challenging, however, when there has been no opportunity to observe, absorb, and learn from positive models for addressing and resolving disagreements and conflicts. Avoiding dealing with important differences out of anticipation of angry reactions only leads to a buildup of resentment over time that can lead to outbursts of rage or ultimately turning away with protective detachment and indifference. So it is gratifying and hopeful when work with couples and families facilitates the development of healthy, respectful, and effective ways of resolving their differences in mutually beneficial ways. I have found that using TFT in couples and family therapy helps to resolve past traumas and hurts, vanquish rage, calm anger, and facilitate healthy communication.

At their initial appointment, Jane and Joe Smith were yelling at each other in the clinic waiting room, causing concern with their out-of-control threats to kill each other. I got to the waiting area and attempted to get their attention by calling their names. It took a few seconds before they finally responded to my invitation to come into my office. They continued their sparring as they came down the hall and sat as far away from each other as my office walls allowed.

I tried to interrupt them a couple of times but quickly realized that any ordinary attempts to get their attention were futile, as they appeared engrossed in a vicious verbal battle for survival. I needed to interrupt them and get them calmed down so we could assess the problems and get them some relief. I started to jump up and down and wave my arms to get their attention, saying I was getting frustrated and wanted to work on finding a solution. They both looked with shock and confusion at the psychologist who seemed to be unpredictable and acting wildly. They stopped momentarily to listen.

I told them I needed to calm myself down and wanted them to join me and follow what I was doing to help me get calmer and more focused again. I started tapping on the side of my hand and asked them to do the same with me to help me so maybe I could help them. That helped all three of us get centered and lessened the negativity and doubt in the room. When Joe and Jane appeared to lower their level of intensity slightly, I then proceeded to tap the rage and anger acupoints on myself while encouraging them to accompany me. I observed Joe and Jane to see that they were both following the TFT algorithms. I commented on getting my frustration and exasperation diminished so we could address what was going on. As they followed the tapping sequences, their energy intensity drop was readily apparent in the decreasing vigor with which they were tapping themselves on the meridian acupoints. They sat back in their chairs with more relaxed shoulders, arms, necks, and now-uncurled fists.

I thanked them for helping me to calm down, and they both laughed and acknowledged that they were themselves markedly more relaxed and realized that the exercise was actually more for their benefit. When asked why they would be threatening to kill each other, they looked at each other with disbelief, as neither could remember what started their fight.

It was readily apparent that everything and anything could trigger an intense power struggle between them. We were then able to have a very productive session on the dynamics of power and control, their family of origin dynamics and influences, traumatic impacts leading to survival defensiveness, and dysfunctional communication patterns.

In subsequent individual and joint sessions, Jane and Joe each worked on the traumatic experiences that predisposed them to overreact when feeling a threat of rejection or abandonment. Joe grew up in a chaotic family with alcoholism, drug abuse, and domestic violence. He had been subjected to physical, verbal, and emotional abuse throughout his formative years.

Joe worked through his various traumas, anger, rage, and resentments. He also addressed his fear of abandonment, which he experienced with his mother and with his girlfriends prior to Jane. He could not forgive his mother for running away from an abusive stepfather who bought his love with many toys and treats. His stepfather was relatively mild in his infrequent anger at Joe, although he had almost killed Joe's mother several times in brutal beatings. Upon addressing his abuse traumas with TFT, Joe gained insights into his relationship problems.

Once he could acknowledge how he drove his girlfriends away with his emotional abuse and threatening behaviors, he was able to work on developing more assertive and effective communication skills to express his needs and fears. His threats and posturing became history in his behavioral repertoire. He related feeling a deep sense of trust and closeness after working through all his issues from his family and personal history and improving his self-concept and self-esteem, which had been shaped and sculpted by his earlier experiences in life.

Jane had a traumatic and painful childhood rife with abuse, losses, and betrayals. She had been raised amidst a rapidly changing family life and had developed strong, unhealthy, dysfunctional beliefs as a result of traumas she had sustained. She had been rejected by her father who questioned paternity and she was later abandoned by her alcoholic mother who defended her second stepfather when Jane attempted to tell her mother about being molested by him. Her mother questioned 7-year-old Jane in an accusatory manner about what she had done to provoke him and said Jane was talking nonsense and would ruin the great life they had since this stepfather was financially solid and could provide amply for their needs.

A classmate reported Jane's plight to a teacher who then filed a report with Child Protective Services. Jane's mother raised questions about Jane's honesty and made up stories about Jane being a chronic liar who fabricated or exaggerated everything. In many ways, this betrayal by her own mother was even more painful for Jane who was feeling hurt, angry, and conflicted about what to say to case workers and investigators. Her conflict intensified after she was removed from the home and turned over to protective custody. Jane recalled her mother's last angry, accusatory words, which were that she wished Jane were dead and that she should never have been born.

Jane became aware of the deep pain and hurt that stemmed from her troubled relationship with her mother. Though their relationship had never been repaired, Jane had finally visited her mother when she learned she was close to death from metastasized cancer. Her mother was slipping in and out of consciousness and did not appear to recognize Jane. But Jane held her mother's hand and told her she forgave her and loved her because she felt it was the proper thing to do, even though she did not really feel that way at the time. In our sessions, she cried profusely with the release of her long-held hurt, rage, and guilt for having those feelings even as her mother lay dying. Jane worked through those pains with TFT for trauma with hurt, anger, and guilt. She had a moving, cathartic, and healing conversation with her deceased mother in an empty chair. Her only wish was that she had worked with TFT earlier, while her mother was still alive and able to communicate.

Jane worked on the traumas with her stepfathers and then with boyfriends and spouses she had prior to Joe, using TFT for trauma and anger, rage, and resentment. She had previously reached the conclusion that all men were alike and realized that she felt bitter toward all men and was taking out her rage and fury on Joe whenever he reminded her of controlling, diminishing, or demeaning behaviors by men in her past. She came to the realization that she so deeply resented what she expected from men that she kept badgering and provoking Joe until he exploded and acted out what he had witnessed and experienced earlier in his own life.

Their dovetailing pathologies kept the vicious cycle going in their relationship as they tried desperately to change the outcomes while repeating the same dysfunctional patterns. Once she was able to overcome her resentment, Jane attained understanding and forgiveness of herself and others, then her perspective of Joe turned around, and she was able to differentiate him from the men in her past.

Both Jane and Joe started to really see each other for the first time. Jane started to truly appreciate Joe's respectful and caring nature. Joe started to keep his commitment to never allow himself to react with violence no matter how angry he felt. Jane shed tears of compassion and joy when she experienced warm regard from Joe and felt profound respect and a deep connection with him that she had never experienced prior to TFT. Healing the wounds of the past opened the pathway for Jane to experience the deep love that she had always dreamed of but had been previously convinced was a cruel illusion that would only bring her further hurt and pain. Some interpersonal therapy added to her understanding and reframing of her relationship perspectives and realizations.

Jane and Joe were determined to break the cycle of violence and power and control. They wanted to have their three children learn to have more meaningful and mutually satisfying relationships with them as well as with their future partners. So they brought their three children in to work through the issues they had developed as a result of their parents' harsh interactions.

John was 11 years old and quickly responded to TFT in working through his anger and underlying anxiety. The bullying behaviors he had exhibited at school ceased. He had taken the brunt of both of his parents' reactions when he repeatedly yelled at them to stop fighting. He physically tried to intervene on several occasions only to have them turn their wrath on him verbally and emotionally. John had been berated to mind his own business and had been scathingly castigated for his bad grades.

Julie was 9 years old and also worked through her trauma and anxiety easily with TFT. In the course of a few sessions, we were able to work through and get past her depression to the underlying hurt and anger. Her mildly withdrawn and depressive behaviors disappeared after the underlying anger and resentment that she had previously dared not express were addressed directly.

Billy was 7 years old and was anxious and fearful of the dark, of crowds, and of large dogs. He curled up in a fetal position with his hands over his ears when his parents fought. His apprehension and anxiety and multiple phobias remitted quickly with TFT for anxiety, trauma, and specific phobias. The marked change in his parents was undoubtedly also a major factor in his rapid response.

All three children had a children's session together, and we looked at problem ownership and how their parents had some issues they had to resolve between themselves. We discussed that those were their parents' problems and that their mom and dad now had the skills and tools to resolve these issues more effectively. The children agreed that their parents were no longer exploding into frightening rages, as they had in the past. John especially realized that he had been trying to intervene in the past because of fears of safety. He was happy that this was no longer needed. John had been acting out his home scenario at school, where his bullying had initially occurred in an effort to help another child who was being picked on and he had gone further than needed, crossing into bullying the bullies.

In a subsequent family session, Joe and Jane started raising their voices a few decibels as their intensity warmed up. I noted movement out of the corner of my eyes and saw the three children spontaneously doing their TFT treatments for trauma. I quickly and quietly got the parents to observe what was happening with their children, and both Joe and Jane immediately realized that raising their voices, even without the verbal threats and gestures, scared the children. Both parents started doing their rage and anger treatments while the three children completed their self-treatments for trauma with broad grins on their faces as they witnessed their parents calming themselves down effectively.

A month later, John related proudly in a follow-up session that he had received a most improved citizenship award at his school and was now participating in a peer-counseling program where he was called upon to talk to an angry, bullying student. He shared his experiences and how he learned to gain control over his emotions and behaviors. He shared that what he was doing now brought him the deep satisfaction of actually being able to help, unlike his previous behaviors that didn't help matters at home or at school and only made things worse for himself. He summed it up aptly, saying that everyone needs to be in control of themselves, respect others, understand others, and then everybody is happier—and it's so easy. Just tap your bad feelings away and think about what you can do to make things better.

Working with families provides an optimal opportunity to make a difference in the life of each member, who can continue to grow positively with the understanding and support of the others in the family. Periodic booster sessions, when needed, can facilitate keeping a family on a healthy track through the different stages of life.

TFT Treatments for Joe

Trauma with Rage and Anger
Eyebrow Under eye Under arm Under collarbone Tiny finger Outside edge of eye Under collarbone 9 Gamut process Repeat acupoint sequence Reversals: side of hand, under nose
Trauma with Resentment and Fear of Abandonment
Side of hand Eyebrow Under eye Under arm Under collarbone Tiny finger Middle finger Under collarbone Under eye Under collarbone 9 Gamut process Repeat acupoint sequence Reversals: tender spot, under nose
Low Self-Esteem and Lack of Self-Confidence
Side of hand Eyebrow Under eye Under arm Under collarbone Index finger Under nose Under lip Under collarbone Under eye Under collarbone 9 Gamut process Repeat acupoint sequence Reversals: tender spot, under nose

TFT Treatments for Jane

Trauma with Hurt, Anger and Guilt
Eyebrow Under eye Under arm Under collarbone Middle finger Tiny finger Index finger Under collarbone 9 Gamut process Repeat acupoint sequence Reversals: side of hand, under nose
Trauma with Rage and Resentment
Eyebrow Under eye Under arm Under collarbone Outside edge of eye Middle finger Tiny finger Under collarbone Under eye Under collarbone 9 Gamut process Repeat acupoint sequence Reversals: side of hand, under nose

TFT Treatments for John

Trauma with Rage

Eyebrow
Under eye
Under arm
Under collarbone
Outside edge of eye
Under collarbone

9 Gamut process
Repeat acupoint sequence
Reversals: side of hand, under nose

Trauma with Anger and Anxiety

Eyebrow
Under eye
Under arm
Under collarbone
Tiny finger
Under collarbone
Under eye
Under collarbone
9 Gamut process
Repeat acupoint sequence
Reversals: side of hand, under nose

TFT Treatments for Julie

Trauma

Eyebrow
Under eye
Under arm
Under collarbone

9 Gamut process
Repeat acupoint sequence
Reversal: side of hand

Anxiety

Under eye
Under arm
Under collarbone

9 Gamut process
Repeat acupoint sequence

Anger with Depression
Tiny finger Under collarbone Gamut spot Under collarbone 9 Gamut process Repeat acupoint sequence Reversal: side of hand

TFT Treatments for Billy

Trauma
Eyebrow Under eye Under arm Under collarbone Reversal: side of hand

Anxiety
Under eye Under arm Under collarbone Reversal: side of hand

Specific Phobias
Under eye Under arm Under collarbone Reversal: side of hand

TRAUMA

13

The Devastating Consequences of PTSD

*For every problem, there exists a solution...and at the very least...
an opportunity.*

—Michael McMillan

Having worked with Rwandan trauma survivors for the past 5 years, also having worked with Katrina first responders and survivors, as well as seeing traumatized individuals in my practice, I have seen several hundred cases of posttraumatic stress disorder (PTSD) in men, children, women, and even animals. The symptoms of PTSD include intrusive flashbacks, nightmares, hyper-reactivity, hyper-startle, avoidance of triggering situations, impaired recall of aspects of the trauma, restricted range of affect, sleep disturbances, irritability, anger outbursts, trouble concentrating, hypervigilance, and numbing out. This next case could be included in all the sections of this book due to the fact that he suffered from so many debilitating effects of combat trauma. Sadly, he lived this way for many years, with devastating consequences, before finally receiving relief.

Sam was a Vietnam combat veteran who was irritable, easily agitated, hypervigilant, and haunted by nightmares and flashbacks of people being killed and threats of his own death. By the time I saw him decades later, he had lost his sense of meaning in life, his wife and family, his jobs, his soul, and his hope.

He began to describe what his life had been like all these years. Before his wife left him, he had physically and verbally terrorized her. He admitted to me that his temper outbursts, intolerance, profanity, and unpredictability had become too much for her. Taking their three children, she left. Sam began drinking even more to numb out the haunting images of death scenes from the war. Nightly, he woke up at various times, drenched in sweat with his heart racing.

Sam's hostile attitude and behavior lost him 19 jobs. With each lost job, it became increasingly difficult to find the next job, given this employment history. He had difficulty getting along with others and blending in, so holding a job was not really possible. He isolated from people and lost all interest in anything that used to give him pleasure. He was also extremely sensitive to noises. He jumped when cars backfired or people raised their voices. He had served his country but came home to experience his life falling apart.

Sam moved from one place to another, seeking help. He had medical issues, which were being assessed and treated. He had been on medication trials, tried exposure therapy, cognitive behavioral therapy, and individual and group treatment, but the symptoms got worse. Just before he came to me, he had moved from his last shelter to living in his car. One day while crossing the street, he was hit by a car and treated at a nearby clinic. The doctor saw his acute PTSD symptoms and referred him to me for psychological treatment.

Sam met PTSD criteria on the two self-report measures he took as well as the structured clinical assessment I administered. He was now avoiding going out and had acute exacerbation of his symptoms. While he desperately wanted help, Sam was hesitant about TFT. He said it sounded strange to him after I briefly explained how it was essentially a self-treatment protocol using acupoints. He was desperate to try anything to get some relief, however, so he followed the tapping sequence I demonstrated on myself and did along with him. He started gingerly tapping the side of his hand, followed by the acupoints for rage and trauma. Sam's tense body and arms shifted into a more relaxed posture. His SUD rating went from a 20 to 7, much to his pleasant surprise. This encouraged him to go further.

We moved on to the next step, the 9 Gamut process, which activates different areas of the brain and is followed by repeating the acupoint sequence. We first checked that he did not have retinal detachment or pain when moving his eyes circularly.

After doing the 9 Gamut process and repeating the acupoint sequence, Sam appeared at ease, with his brow unfurrowed and his shoulders loosened. He reported, with a hint of a smile, that his SUD was now at 5. He eagerly found his lymphatic drainage point, the tender spot, to massage briefly and gently (see Appendix A). This reversal point is often used when there are recurrent symptoms. We then repeated the entire treatment protocol: acupoint sequence, 9 Gamut process, acupoint sequence. He smiled broadly as he reported that his SUD level had dropped to 3.

He followed as we tapped ourselves under the nose and repeated the treatment protocol of acupoint sequence, 9 Gamut process, acupoint sequence. Sam now broke into a huge grin as he stated with disbelief that his SUD score was down to 1. As he thought at length about the accident, he could feel some tension, but now it was at SUD 2 rather than 20.

In subsequent sessions, Sam worked further on what the accident had triggered and used peak performance (see Appendix E) to enhance his confidence to walk outside and cross streets without overwhelming fear. In the series of sessions that followed, we focused on the war traumas that had never left him and had intensified with the accident.

Sam felt the spring coming back into his step along with his hope to have a life post Vietnam, after all these years. He reported several incidents in which situations and people around him triggered him and how he tapped himself to calm the emotional storms. Sam described himself as a work in progress, saying that he'll need to tap often for his stability and health. He experienced a sense of relief and joy that, for decades, had seemed unattainable and foreign to him. Sam enthusiastically shared his experience with fellow veterans and persuaded several of them who were haunted by their memories and trapped in that mental hell to get relief with TFT and counseling services, as he had done.

TFT Treatments for Sam

Overwhelm with Trauma, Rage, Anger and Ruminating Thoughts

Side of hand
Outside edge of eye
Tiny finger Eyebrow
Under eye
Under arm
Under collarbone
Under eye
Under collarbone

9 Gamut process
Repeat acupoint sequence

Trauma with Anger, Rage, Overwhelm, Embarrassment, Shame, and Ruminating Thoughts

Eyebrow
Under eye
Under arm
Under collarbone
Tiny finger
Outside edge of eye
Under nose
Under lip
Under collarbone
Under eye
Under collarbone

9 Gamut process
Repeat acupoint sequence
Reversal: side of hand

Guilt and Trauma with Ruminating Thoughts

Index finger
Under collarbone
Eyebrow
Under eye
Under arm
Under collarbone
Under eye
Under collarbone

9 Gamut process
Repeat acupoint sequence
Reversal: side of hand

14

Overcoming the Unthinkable

The significant problems we face cannot be solved at the same level of thinking we were at when we created them.

—Albert Einstein

Sexual trauma has been depicted by many of my clients who have experienced both physical and sexual abuse as having deeper and longer-lasting effects on their self-concept, self-esteem, and emotional well-being. They felt they recovered much more quickly from physical injuries, but the confusion, hurt, disgust, revulsion, resentment, rage, anger, fear, and guilt from sexual abuse remained like open wounds. They felt unable to clean them up and clear them out of their minds and memories.

While physical injuries from violent sexual assaults heal within a predictable time frame, the psychological and emotional wounds can take a much longer and more variable course. The prior history and internal resources of the person affects resilience. Support and external resources can facilitate healing and, as more efficient ways of helping those who remain trapped in reliving their traumas are developed and validated by empirical studies, it is important for helping professionals to learn about them.

For over 10 years, Krista had tried many times to escape the haunting memories of a terrifying rape that left her fearful for life. She had been told that she had intractable PTSD because the debilitating symptoms of trauma continued unabated from the brutal rape and her childhood history of sexual abuse. She was fearful, hypervigilant, and suffered from haunting flashbacks on incessant replay. Krista dreaded falling asleep only to be attacked repeatedly all over again in her unrelenting nightmares. She had continued to struggle for so many years because TFT, Energy Psychology, and other newer treatment approaches were overlooked and even dismissed as treatment options, though the conventional approaches were not yielding any relief of her debilitating symptoms.

The criminal trial was paradoxically a curse and a blessing. She endured having to repeat the horrifying details in the courtroom but only because she wanted her assaulter off the street so he could harm her no more. The intrusive and jarring questions often felt like intrusive probes and daggers. Krista had hoped that when the onerous trial was finally over, she could put the ordeal behind her. Although she was relieved that the rapist was sentenced for an extended incarceration in prison, she was discouraged and disappointed when the flashbacks and nightmares relentlessly continued.

Over the years, Krista continued to feel the effects of PTSD, which sadly alienated her from any healthy support. Whenever anyone mentioned they were sorry for what she had suffered, she felt an intensification of her pain—physical and emotional. She stated that she felt electrocuted by the memory waves, which constantly zapped her mind, body, and spirit. She had fallen away from her faith because she could not trust a god that let such unspeakable evils happen in the world. Her family and friends were initially sympathetic and understanding, but as the years went on, they began to question why she "wasn't getting over it" and that she should "move on with her life." Unfortunately, their lack of understanding of the individualized healing-process time line and their expressing impatience and frustration made Krista's recovery even more difficult, as she felt alone, unsupported, misunderstood, and that she was a failure and disappointment to her family and friends. In their exasperation and feelings of helplessness to render any relief from her agonies, some even implied that she might be holding on to her painful memories for attention. This really bewildered and hurt her. Who would ever choose such an insane action if they had any choice in the matter?

Krista sought help from several psychiatrists and psychologists, but her flashbacks and nightmares continued to haunt her. She kept going to therapy in the slim hopes of someday recovering from her trauma. On the contrary, her symptoms only intensified with the retelling of the rape. Her visual, auditory, tactile, and olfactory memories would also be triggered. She came to dread her therapy appointments simply due to the fact that they seemed to trigger more nightmares. She felt the positive intentions of her therapists, but nothing was changing.

Among her friends were three women who themselves had been through traumatic experiences. They had each found TFT to be most helpful in healing from the wounds of their traumas, and they strongly believed that it would also help Krista. When she finally hesitantly called, I suggested that since she was in ongoing psychotherapy at the time, she should ask her current therapist for clearance to have a consultation (one to three sessions) to learn TFT self-treatments to help her with symptom management, and I could share information about TFT with her therapist if that would be helpful in considering this. Her therapist was not familiar with TFT, declined the offer to learn about it, and discouraged Krista from having the consultation.

Another year passed with Krista trying to get relief from her symptoms. As a gift, her three friends gave her a consultation session with me. This time, Krista made the appointment and came in to appease her girlfriends, who were insistent that she try this therapy. Krista showed up with skepticism and low expectations that anything would come of the session. This was understandable after years of having her hopes elevated and then dashed again when nothing seemed to remit her haunting and terrifying experiences.

After a brief explanation of TFT and some examples of how it has helped with PTSD, she was willing to try it out. Her SUD rating was 10 as she focused on the traumatic images that were ever-present. As she tapped on the acupoints I demonstrated by tapping on myself, she looked perplexed and confused as she found the intrusive images harder to keep in focus. As her SUD score dropped to 5, then 3, then 1 to 0 with each next step in her treatment protocol, her bewilderment transformed into relief and elation at the difference she felt. She described how the vivid, bigger-than-life flashbacks receded into the past as she tapped on the acupoints. She felt hope for the first time since her ordeal and felt the start of her transformation from helpless victim to being back in control of her life. She felt peace and achieved a respite from her unrelenting nightmares for the first time.

At her follow-up appointment, she related that she was no longer haunted by the rape trauma, but earlier memories of childhood incest and physical abuse were now coming up, and she wished to work on those memories. The intensities of those memories were lower than the rape trauma, starting at SUD 6 and dropping to 4, 2, 1, 0.5, then 0 with the reversals used with the trauma with guilt and sadness treatment protocol.

Earlier traumas stored in the mind-body system are often reactivated by more recent traumatic events. When these underlying traumatic layers were subsequently addressed and treated with TFT, to Krista's amazement, all her emotional, physical, and mental symptoms abated. She wept tears of relief and joy, as she never thought she could recover from all that she had endured. Krista related that she had felt so disempowered by the traumatic events in her life that she previously could not even imagine that she would ever feel empowered again. She felt back in control of her life, her thoughts, her memories, her feelings, and now her future without the debilitating symptoms of PTSD.

Her gratitude propelled her to help a relative who had been traumatized with multiple childhood abuses and who was also stuck in terror and grief. Krista said she not only felt empowered herself, but was also elated that she could help to empower others with TFT.

TFT Treatments for Krista

Overwhelm with Trauma, Rage, and Guilt
Side of hand Eyebrow Under eye Under arm Under collarbone Outside edge of eye Index finger Under collarbone 9 Gamut process Repeat acupoint sequence Reversals: tender spot, under nose
Trauma with Guilt and Sadness
Eyebrow Under eye Under arm Under collarbone Index finger Under collarbone Gamut spot Under collarbone 9 Gamut process Repeat acupoint sequence Reversals: side of hand, tender spot, under nose

COMPLEX ISSUES

15

From Dissociation to Integration

So many of our dreams at first seem impossible, then they seem improbable, and then when we summon the will, they become inevitable.

—Christopher Reeve

In the past, many symptoms that might have been reactions to and adaptations to trauma have been stigmatized as mental disorders. Looking at the devastating, complex, far-reaching, and long-lasting effects of trauma and the possibilities of reversing those consequences brings a much more hopeful view and perspective. We are not just our history; we are not determined solely by our genetics or our past. We can make choices to have healthier attitudes and develop more functional and positive states and eventually traits.

Upon first meeting Sasha, my general impression was that she was a bright young woman who immediately needed help. She had come in for treatment on the referral of her primary care physician who was concerned about Sasha's agitation surrounding a man who insisted that they had shared some significant experiences. Sasha was convinced that she had never met him before. As she described what was going on with her, it became evident that she had endured a lot over her lifetime.

Sasha had periods of time she could not account for, which caused her confusion and concern. She worried about what she might have done or said when people she did not recognize told her that they had met her before. All were astonished that she did not have the foggiest recollection of them. She had been startled to find strange and unusual clothes in her closet that were not anything like what she would buy or wear according to her conservative tastes and fashion preferences. She was even more confused over bills for bizarre items that she had supposedly bid for on the Internet. She was also accused of flirting with the boyfriend of a female acquaintance who, as a result of Sasha's flirting, no longer wanted to be friends. But Sasha declared that she had absolutely no interest or attraction to this gentleman and would not make seductive comments, as she was highly moral and even teased by some of her acquaintances as a prude. Most of the time, she didn't have any clue as to why people were upset with her. She felt exasperated that they wouldn't tell her anything, implying that she should know what she did.

During the intake session, Sasha revealed that she couldn't recall several time periods in her childhood, adolescence, and adult life. She knew where she lived during these different time periods and where she went to school but had only spotty recollections. As she tried to piece things together, she remembered being terrified much of the time after her father died when she was 2 years old. Her distraught mother took out her anger and frustration on Sasha and her siblings. Sasha often cried herself to sleep after being beaten with brooms, hairbrushes, and hangers. She was called ugly names and told that she was worthless and that she would never amount to anything. Although Sasha made mostly A's in school and never got into trouble in the classroom, her self-esteem and sense of worth were dismal. She kept trying to prove to her mother that she was worthy, to no avail. As a result, she felt she was wrong or not good enough or too late in everything she did.

Sasha scored high in the screening assessments for dissociative disorders and exhibited signs and symptoms in her clinical interviews. She was motivated and committed to following through with strengthening her internal and external resources, developing more effective coping strategies, and doing the longer-term integrative work that was indicated. Selected aspects of this extended treatment over almost 2 years are briefly summarized here.

Sasha worked with TFT on her trauma, anger, resentment, and guilt regarding her mother. Her tears and anguish changed into smiles and feelings of pride for what she had accomplished (graduating from high school and going on to graduate from college), despite much opposition and many obstacles. Her mother had not only yelled at her repeatedly for being stupid, but also berated her for wasting her time and money studying when she could be getting a job and earning money instead.

In using TFT to work through her hurt and anger at the daily abuses by her mother, she became aware of a deeper layer of resentment and trauma that she had successfully blocked for years. She painfully recalled haltingly telling her mother about her stepfather touching her inappropriately when she was around 5 years old. She does not remember much before then except that she tried to hide from him whenever she could. Her mother often worked in the evenings, during which time he controlled and terrorized the children. Sasha believed she was the only one who tried to tell their mother and felt ashamed when she was yelled at for being a bad girl for not sitting properly with her knees together.

Despite gathering the courage to confide in her mother, Sasha was made to feel that her stepfather touching her was her fault. She did not realize that her mother's blaming her was a way of avoiding devastating self-blame for not ensuring her daughter's safety and well-being and for being responsible for actually bringing a predator into Sasha's life. This is commonly encountered with sexual abuse, which complicates matters, as the child feels confused and is made to feel guilty about the conflict and, in some instances, even made to feel competitive with her parent. She may be blamed for what happened and then coopted into silence about what is occurring in the dysfunctional family system.

We did extensive TFT work along with interpersonal therapy, Gestalt therapy, and cognitive reframing with positive self-statements for healing this hurt and shame. As Sasha worked on the heart-wrenching emotional pain of her mother not protecting her and instead blaming her as a bad child who caused the behaviors of her stepfather, she started to feel nauseous. She began to recall the revolting things that her stepfather did to her over the years from when she was a toddler until she was an older teenager. Sasha worked on her multiple traumas as they came to her awareness, and the physical symptoms she had carried for decades began to abate for the first time: her medically unexplained abdominal pains, episodes of racing heartbeats for no apparent reasons, her gagging reflex without a medical reason, and her disturbing bouts of nausea that defied medical diagnoses.

Over time with the TFT work, Sasha's dissociative episodes of losing time and awareness started to diminish in length and frequency. She stopped finding things that she could not recall purchasing or doing, such as drawings or writings that she did not remember creating. Sasha started to feel that she was now actually living in her body—with her body and mind getting together and synchronizing. Previously, she had described herself as feeling like two separate entities with no central control and no integration. Now she felt she was discovering who she was for the first time, and although initially she felt some confusion and feelings of uncertainty, it was profoundly more reassuring to feel integrated as one mind-body and body-mind rather than feeling disconnected and locked outside of parts of her own awareness.

She worked through her revulsion for the male gender and could clearly see her stepfather's manipulations and abusive behaviors without feeling guilty about her tomboyish behaviors as a young child. Sasha could understand and forgive herself for her subsequent counter-attempts at control by using her sexuality to manipulate her stepfather once she realized his addictions. She could see that her detachment and dissociation allowed her to survive her multileveled abuses by her stepfather and mother, and she developed ways to have some semblance of control in an intolerable situation. These traumatic episodes and her ensuing survival through dissociative blanking out led to gaps in her growth as a human being in various levels and layers of her development. Sasha began her journey into defining herself and learning what her likes and dislikes were, and developing awareness and skills that had been blocked by her traumatic and dissociative experiences. Interpersonal therapy and dialectical behavior therapy augmented by Energy Psychology helped her in integrating and clarifying herself and building needed skills.

Sasha discovered her passion for helping others, and she volunteered to be of service in church ministries, helping nonprofit organizations, and aiding the elderly and disabled individuals in her community. She contributed her time and knowledge with compassion while being able to set clear boundaries and limits and maintaining a healthy balance between her efforts to help others and her own personal life, needs, and goals.

TFT Treatments for Sasha

Trauma with Anger, Hurt, Guilt, and Obsessive Thoughts
Eyebrow
Under eye
Under arm
Under collarbone
Tiny finger
Middle finger
Index finger
Under collarbone
Under eye
Under collarbone
9 Gamut process
Repeat acupoint sequence
Reversals: side of hand, tender spot, index finger, under nose

Trauma with Anger, Guilt, and Sadness
Eyebrow
Under eye
Under arm
Under collarbone
Tiny finger
Index finger
Gamut spot
Under collarbone
9 Gamut process
Repeat acupoint sequence
Reversals: side of hand, under nose

Trauma with Rage and Overwhelm
Side of hand Eyebrow Under eye Under arm Under collarbone Outside edge of eye Under collarbone Side of hand 9 Gamut process Repeat acupoint sequence Reversals: tender spot, index finger, under nose

Trauma with Hurt and Anger
Eyebrow Under eye Under arm Under collarbone Middle finger Tiny finger Under collarbone 9 Gamut process Repeat acupoint sequence Reversals: side of hand, under nose

Anxiety
Under eye Under arm Under collarbone 9 Gamut process Repeat acupoint sequence Reversals: side of hand, tender spot, under nose

16

The Invisible Shell of a Child

Skill to do comes of doing.

—Ralph Waldo Emerson

We generally let others know our needs and feelings and gain understanding and clarity about them through our spoken communication. Children and adults who don't have verbal communication present special challenges. TFT can aid in accessing information stored in the body's energy system, helping the individual work through traumas and blocks without necessarily requiring the verbal descriptors or history. Traumatic events can freeze and lock individuals into that earlier time period, and releasing those traumatic states can facilitate recovery, growth, and maturation.

Bunny lived in her own little 2-year-old world. She didn't speak words—only cried or yelled anguished sounds, struck out physically in fury, or withdrew into her invisible shell. She had been adopted from an Asian orphanage as an infant, and her birth parents were unknown, as Bunny had been abandoned. She had very caring adoptive parents who were delighted at getting Bunny and lavished on her a lot of love, attention, patience, and all the material comforts and luxuries a child could want. They were saddened to find out that her social, mental, and emotional developmental levels were falling behind expected norms and that she had been diagnosed with a developmental disability in the autistic spectrum.

We began with the plan to teach TFT to her parents and Bunny's caretaker and behavioral therapist. I explained to the significant adults in her life about TFT in simplified language that the 2-year-old could readily understand while she played with a toy nearby. When I started showing the adults what the different treatment points for rage and anger were and we started tapping together, Bunny watched intently out of the corners of her eyes. When we addressed how it could be done with Bunny, I looked at Bunny and said she could tap herself if she chose to or one of her adult caregivers could do it by gently massaging the acupoints on both sides of the body (there are two of every TFT acupoint, one on each side of the body). This is known as bilateral massage—gently rubbing both acupoints simultaneously. Bunny responded by tapping on herself, which was an unexpected positive and collaborative response.

Bunny's rages had become hazardous, as she struck people repeatedly and rapidly with all the force her little body could muster, as if fighting for her life. Because of her tiny stature, she often hit people in sensitive areas, and they subsequently avoided close contact with her if they did not have to be engaged in her life. It was nearly impossible to find suitable caretakers for her when her parents were working or needed to go out without her.

Noting that Bunny was striking out at people with both blades of her hands (Karate Chop points), I got her a large overstuffed toy alligator that we called Ally, her anger alligator. When introducing Ally to Bunny, I explained that Ally liked a thumping massage on his back to calm himself and others down. Her parents and I told Bunny firmly that it was not okay to hit people because they could get hurt—unlike Ally, who was happy to get a thumping because he liked to get calm and calm people down too. Bunny vigorously hit Ally with the blades of her hands. This got Bunny centered and focused. She then was able to do the rest of her anger and rage algorithm, and her pounding heart calmed; the tension in her arms, legs, and torso diminished; and the storm within quieted down. Her reduction in tension was readily apparent, with her fists relaxing, her cocked arms straightening, and her head elongating out of her now-dropped shoulders. Her breathing also spontaneously slowed.

Both parents, her caretaker, and her behavioral therapist generally did the treatments along with Bunny. When she was not activating the TFT acupoints herself, they used bilateral massage on Bunny's acupoints as best they could. Bunny started to be able to focus more on learning and speaking, as time and energy were not being depleted by her rage episodes.

Bunny apparently had a vocabulary that she had never before voiced but had understood and was now able to articulate. She started saying no and could now say she was mad, sad, happy, or needing something. Her frustration level markedly decreased with her ability to express her wants and needs in words.

We later began to treat what we assumed might be some form of past trauma by doing the trauma with anger and rage protocol when she was in a state of rage. Bunny started crying, thrashing her arms, kicking her legs, shivering intensely, and her whole body shook with sobs. Then suddenly, she said, "Light, light," and ceased her thrashing. We were not sure what all this meant, but she had been found abandoned under a well-traveled bridge. An early morning jogger heard a baby's frantic cry and had found her cold, wet, and shivering in a basket, as the rising sun illuminated her face and hands.

Bunny continued to progress over time in her speaking to more people, and her learning accelerated with her increased interactions and decreased disruptive rages. She was responsive to her special-education coach and took pride in what she was learning. Her rages ceased as she regularly and spontaneously used her self-regulation skills. She had sadness when disappointed and anger when frustrated in doing something challenging for her, and she responded to algorithms for those emotions, which she now voiced in words rather than tantrum behaviors. Four years later, her delighted parents beamed as Bunny was initiated into a mainstream educational class.

Since then, Bunny's parents have reached out to other struggling parents to share their experiences, show them some of the TFT treatments they found most helpful, and connecting them with further help. They both do a lot of advocacy for children with special needs, the Special Olympics, and other humanitarian and charitable causes.

TFT Treatments for Bunny

Psychological Reversal/Centering
Side of hand

Rage and Anger
Side of hand Tiny finger Outside edge of eye Under collarbone Repeat acupoint sequence

Trauma with Rage and Anger
Side of hand Eyebrow Under eye Under arm Under collarbone Outside edge of eye Tiny finger Under collarbone Repeat acupoint sequence as needed

Sadness
Gamut spot Under collarbone Repeat acupoint sequence as needed

Anger and Stress
Tiny finger Under eye Under arm Under collarbone Repeat acupoint sequence as needed

PHYSICAL PAIN

17

From Painful to Playful

We make a living by what we get. We make a life by what we give.
—Winston Churchill

Physical pain can be caused by physical injury, trauma, or medical conditions. Medications can numb the pain, and distractions of various types can shift the focus of attention to lessen the felt intensity of the pain. Stress, anger, rage, obsessive thoughts, fears, depression, and anxiety can exacerbate the symptoms of pain. TFT can help with reducing the emotions that exacerbate the pain symptoms as well as give the sufferer tools to manage the pain directly and help treat the stored somatic memories of pain related to trauma.

Jillian hobbled into my office with a pained grimace. She was depressed and angry following a motor vehicle accident while on the job. An inattentive driver in a truck had rear-ended her while she was stopped at a red light. This caused her car to hit the car in front of her. Rather than being apologetic, the truck driver yelled at her for being an inept female driver and was joined by the male driver from the car in front of her. No one even asked if she was all right. She was stunned speechless and was close to tears then, but felt indignation and rage later as she recovered from the shock of the accident.

She sustained whiplash in her neck and fractures and dislocations in her lower and mid-back that made it painful to move for several weeks. She was irate that her employer seemed more concerned about the totaled vehicle than her physical and emotional condition, and he kept asking when she was going to return to work. She dreaded even the thought of driving again and found herself obsessively scanning the rearview mirror in fear of being hit again when she drove down the street to the grocery store.

After learning about TFT, she first worked on her rage and anger about the accident. Jillian realized that the rage tensed the muscles in her entire body and aggravated the pain in her neck, back, and legs, but she had been unable to stop the angry, obsessive thoughts and triggering images. I could see her body relax considerably as she tapped her anger down from a SUD rating of 10 to 5 and then to 0. She remarked with surprise that her pain had dropped from 8 to 7 even though we had not worked directly on the pain yet. As we tapped next on the acupoints for trauma and pain, her SUD level dropped from 7 to 5, then down to 4, 2, 1, and 0.5.

Jillian left with a spring in her step and a more erect posture. She continued doing her self-treatments and was able to resume all her household chores. She decided to change to a different job, as she didn't enjoy driving as much as her job demanded. She was able to drive herself to and from work without undue hypervigilance, but she was alert and drove defensively, trying to protect herself from the drivers around her. Jillian was elated that she could once again enjoy hiking and swimming, joys she had thought she would never be able to enjoy again.

Jillian referred a neighbor who had suffered from pain and trauma following a motor vehicle accident, a relative with anger issues, and a friend who had chronic pain from her medical conditions for help with TFT, and each came in ready to try what they had seen turn Jillian's pain and anger around.

TFT Treatments for Jillian

Rage, Anger, and Obsessive Thoughts
Side of hand Outside edge of eye Tiny finger Under collarbone Under eye Under collarbone 9 Gamut process Repeat acupoint sequence

Trauma and Pain
Side of hand Eyebrow Under eye Under arm Under collarbone Gamut spot Under collarbone 9 Gamut process Repeat acupoint sequence Reversals: tender spot, index finger, under nose

18

From Can't Stand to Can Manage

Individual commitment to a group effort—that is what makes a team work, a company work, a society work, a civilization work.

—Vincent Thomas Lombardi

Wanting to wean Gordon off his pain medication of several years, his primary care physician referred him to me. The pain had been chronic since a motor vehicle accident 8 years before, which had been exacerbated by a fall 4 years ago. Gordon was a tall mid-life gentleman who hobbled in with a cane and a pained expression and with a hunched-over posture that made him appear a foot shorter than he was. His gait was laborious and stiff and his range of motion limited, although his doctor reported that all his multiple injuries from the accident and fall had healed well.

Gordon shared in vivid detail what he recalled from the accident, relating it graphically with sights, sounds, smells, and physical sensations as if it had just happened hours ago. He lamented that he relived it often in his nightmares, which caused him to startle awake. He realized that the pain medication had not only been helpful in numbing his physical pain, but also in giving him a reprieve from the constant emotional distress. The flashbacks and nightmares, however, continued unabated and triggered the physical pain when he tensed up and unrelentingly relived the accident.

Initially, Gordon wanted a second opinion, as he wanted to continue on his pain medication. Once he accepted that was not my role as a psychologist but that we could work with different treatments to see what could help him to manage the pain better, he was open to trying TFT.

We used the standard pain algorithm and the trauma algorithm with all the reversals (see appendices B and C). His SUD rating on the traumas went from 10 down to 7 to 3 to 1 to 0. His pain SUD score went from 10 to 8 to 6 to 4 to 2 to 0. Subsequently, Gordon worked on his addiction to pain medication. Having alternative ways to manage the pain, he was able to bring down his craving and worked with his physician to taper off the medication gradually over several weeks.

He summed it up best by stating that he went from "I can't stand the pain" to "I can manage the pain" to "What pain?" He progressed from "I can't stop taking these pills" to "I can do it" to "I did it!" He offered help to his good friend who was addicted to pain medications, sharing his story, convincing his friend to give it a try, and then supporting him by tapping with him once his friend got into therapy. Gordon related that it was further empowering to help his friend and doing the energy treatment together also reinforced his mastery of his own pain management.

TFT Treatments for Gordon

Chronic Pain

Gamut spot
Under collarbone

9 Gamut process
Repeat acupoint sequence
Reversals: side of hand, tender spot, index finger, under nose

Trauma

Eyebrow
Under eye
Under arm
Under collarbone

9 Gamut process
Repeat acupoint sequence
Reversals: side of hand, tender spot, index finger, under nose

Addiction

Side of hand
Under eye
Under arm
Under collarbone

9 Gamut process
Repeat acupoint sequence
Reversals: tender spot, index finger, under nose, collarbone
    breathing

19

The Power of
the Group

*There are many ways of moving forward, but only one way
of standing still.*

—Franklin Roosevelt

According to the American Pain Foundation, an estimated 50 million Americans suffer from some type of persistent pain. From headaches to back pain to arthritis to fibromyalgia, there is no doubt that chronic pain is an epidemic. The sources of pain are too numerous to get into here; however, all people suffering from chronic pain have to devote time in their lives to dealing with their ailments. Pain also interferes with social life and has been linked to depression.

Marlene had intractable pain for a decade after a medical procedure that went awry. She reported pain from her toes to the top of her head, with the most intense pain in her head, abdomen, throat, arms, and legs. She rated her pain at 10 on the SUD scale. The pain interfered with her sleep, allowing her only about 3 hours of sleep a night. She suffered from depression, secondary to the pain and the limitations it placed on her work, marital, and social functioning.

A motor vehicle accident from 20 years prior had resulted in a coma and traumatic brain injury, from which she had recovered over time. Compared to her more recent medical trauma, Marlene's recovery progress from the accident was rapid and complete.

After the medical procedure, Marlene had been worked up for possible chronic regional pain syndrome, traumatic brain injury, and sensory peripheral neuropathy. Medical evaluations revealed mild degenerative changes, mild diffuse disc bulges with mild posterior disc protrusion and degenerative spondylitic changes, mild broad-based posterior disc protrusion, and innumerable hepatic cysts.

Like many pain sufferers, Marlene had tried every possible technique and medication to try and relieve her pain: anesthetic blocks, steroid injections, heat/ice, acupuncture, massage, physical therapy, yoga, meditation, imagery, relaxation exercises, stretching, TENS unit, ultrasound, aqua therapy, traction, distraction, trigger point injections, prayer, and hypnosis. She had been on Oxycontin, Tegretol, Neurontin, Cymbalta, Lyrica, Provigil, Keppra, fentanyl, methadone, Phenergan, Ambien, and Actiq. She had been on narcotics, opiates, antidepressants, anti-inflammatory medications, and sleeping pills. She had reactions to sulfa meds, triptan drugs, Celebrex, PCN, Stadol, Vioxx, Zomig, Vicodin, Tylenol with codeine, and Bextra.

Marlene's neurologist referred her to me. In our session, Marlene reported vertigo, difficulty swallowing, shortness of breath and tightness in her chest, gastrointestinal symptoms, constipation, urinary hesitancy, intolerance to cold, difficulty concentrating, irritability, memory difficulties, mood swings, sleep disturbances, and night sweats. She complained that she suffered from "dead days" during which she could not function. She had intrusive recollections, hyper-startle, flashbacks, and avoidance behaviors, and met the criteria for PTSD.

Marlene reported no appreciable results with any of the listed interventions and treatments, including being on eight to 10 different medications concurrently in attempts to manage her pain. Her first substantive relief was with TFT when, to her amazement, she dropped from SUD 10 to 7 with treatments of trauma, pain, anger, frustration, and stress. She did TFT treatments at home to manage the pain but reported that she had more profound effects in my office where she had gotten her SUD level down to as low as 4 in a number of her sessions.

In Rwanda, our Association for Thought Field Therapy trauma relief team had seen the enhanced power of TFT with additional practitioners tapping together with the treating practitioner and client. The Rwandans had done this spontaneously to lend support where they felt it might be needed. This may have explained why Marlene experienced better results in my office. I shared this with Marlene and her husband, who raised the question about what else could be done to enhance her treatment because, at this point, they had stopped searching for alternatives.

Marlene had always done her TFT treatments privately at home. We discussed having her husband join her in doing the treatments, and we'd get other TFT practitioners who might be willing to help in this trial of group-support enhancement of TFT effects. Four TFT practitioners volunteered and, with safeguards for confidentiality addressed, we met for a group trial of TFT.

Marlene, her husband, the four other TFT practitioners, and I sat in a circle and started tapping on ourselves in unison, using the treatment sequences I had identified for Marlene through the TFT diagnostic procedure to determine the acupoints needing to be activated. We all witnessed Marlene experiencing a profound shift. The color in her face changed and her posture shifted. She reported "a wave of release" and tears ran down her face. She is generally not an emotional individual, and she and her husband shared how unusual it was for her to feel and express such strong emotions.

She said incredulously that her SUD level had gone down to 2, which she had not imagined would be possible for her. Marlene reported a sensation of energy "blending" and diffusing throughout her entire body. She said it was the "best rush" she's ever felt and had not felt that good or happy since before the procedure that went awry. The effects lasted for an hour, and a still-reduced SUD of 4 to 5 lasted until the middle of the next day, which she had not experienced with anything else. She reported having fewer and less intense "dead days" since the group intervention.

On a follow-up group-support treatment, her original pain went down to SUD 0. She can function more effectively with her pain being better managed due to her TFT treatments. She is working on identification of retriggering individualized energy sensitivities, working with the pulse test by Dr. Arthur Coca (see Appendix F) and TFT diagnostic testing, as well as her own systematic checking of suspected triggers.

Marlene has now established a virtual team at home, consisting of her family members in another state, her husband, and herself working together on Skype, with videos of the treatment algorithms from treatment sessions filmed by her husband playing simultaneously. She reported that not only does she get deeper and longer-lasting results than when she does the treatments solo, but also her virtual team members report that they too feel more relaxed and are sleeping better! Marlene has enthusiastically and persuasively shared with friends and acquaintances the transformative experiences that have helped her resume her normal life and work, and she has helped them discover how Energy Psychology methods can enhance their lives and functioning.

TFT Treatments for Marlene

> **Note:** Some of the individually assessed TFT diagnostic sequences had some additional points and some slight variations but were similar to the simplified combined algorithms listed—what is important is the specific sequence and order of the meridian acupoints that may or may not be related to the algorithm name. For example, the person might have described feelings of anger, but if the diagnosed meridian acupoints were the ones typically found by Dr. Callahan for rage, the component is referred to as the rage algorithm (see Appendix C).

Overwhelm with Trauma, Anger, Rage, and Pain

Side of hand
Eyebrow
Under eye
Under nose
Under arm
Under collarbone
Tiny finger
Outside edge of eye
Gamut spot
Under collarbone

9 Gamut process
Repeat acupoint sequence
Reversals: tender spot, index finger, under nose

Trauma with Anger, Pain, Hurt, and Embarrassment

Eyebrow
Under eye
Under arm
Under collarbone
Tiny finger
Gamut spot
Middle finger
Under collarbone
Under nose

9 Gamut process
Repeat acupoint sequence

Trauma with Depression and Frustration
Eyebrow Under eye Under arm Under collarbone Reversals: side of hand, tender spot, index finger, under nose

Trauma with Depression and Frustration
Under eye Under arm Under collarbone Gamut spot Tiny finger Under eye Under arm Under collarbone 9 Gamut process Repeat acupoint sequence Reversals: side of hand, tender spot, index finger, under nose

Trauma with Sadness, Anger, and Guilt
Eyebrow Under eye Under arm Under collarbone Gamut spot Tiny finger Index finger Under collarbone 9 Gamut process Repeat acupoint sequence Reversals: side of hand, tender spot, index finger, under nose

Anger and Rage with Hurt, Guilt, and Trauma

Tiny finger
Outside edge of eye
Under collarbone
Middle finger
Tiny finger
Index finger
Eyebrow
Under eye
Under arm
Under collarbone

9 Gamut process
Repeat acupoint sequence
Reversals: side of hand, tender spot, index finger, under nose

Pain with Anger, Hurt, Shame, and Embarrassment

Gamut spot
Tiny finger
Middle finger
Under lip
Under nose
Under collarbone

9 Gamut process
Repeat acupoint sequence
Reversals: side of hand, tender spot, index finger, under nose

Trauma with Pain and Obsessive Perfectionism

Eyebrow
Under eye
Under arm
Under collarbone
Gamut spot
Tiny finger
Index finger
Under collarbone

9 Gamut process
Repeat acupoint sequence
Reversals: side of hand, tender spot, index finger, under nose

Trauma with Rage, Hurt, and Obsessive Thinking
Eyebrow Under eye Under arm Under collarbone Outside edge of eye Middle finger Under collarbone Under eye Under collarbone 9 Gamut process Repeat acupoint sequence Reversals: side of hand, tender spot, index finger, under nose

Depression with Hurt, Anxiety, and Obsessive Worry
Gamut spot Under collarbone Middle finger Under eye Under arm Under collarbone Under eye Under collarbone 9 Gamut process Repeat acupoint sequence Reversals: side of hand, tender spot, index finger, under nose

Dr. Arthur Coca's pulse test and log (see Appendix F).

Part II
Stories of Rwandan Healing

Introduction:
TFT in Rwanda

Nonviolence is not a garment to be put on and off at will. Its seat is in the heart, and it must be an inseparable part of our being.

—Mahatma Gandhi

In the 1994 genocide in Rwanda, more than 850,000 men, women, and children were massacred within a hundred days. A horrific and unspeakable tragedy, only bits and pieces of information were reported outside the country as it was occurring, and to this day, all the complexities of the traumas, wars, and background events are not fully understood. It is complicated and not something I would even attempt to relate; I will leave that to historical scholars. What is clear is that everyone in the country was affected by the large-scale traumas over the years during and following these tragic events. This called for ways to help with large-scale trauma where health-professional resources were limited and the needs were vast.

In 2006, I received an invitation through Dr. Paul Oas from El Shaddai (now the Rwandan Orphans Project Center for Street Children) to help with the treatment of the persistent behavioral and emotional symptoms of post-genocide orphans who had been brought in from the streets to this transitional school and orphanage. I led a clinical team of TFT volunteer practitioners, which was sponsored by the Association for TFT (ATFT) Foundation Trauma Relief Committee. We were aware that these children had been living with their symptoms of trauma for 12 years already. There were 174 genocide survivors among the 400 children housed in an old abandoned warehouse that served as home for the boys and day school for both boys and girls.

Before we arrived, we were briefed on what to expect. We were told that the children suffered from a multitude of symptoms associated with chronic PTSD: nightmares; day-mares (flashbacks); reliving the horrors of the massacre of their families, neighbors, and friends; jumpiness (hyper-startle); depression; withdrawal; isolation; difficulty concentrating; anger; rage; mistrust; resentment; fear; anxiety; phobias; chronic pain; headaches; bed-wetting; and aggression.

The most severely traumatized genocide survivors, as rated on a PTSD assessment scale by their teachers and guardians, were seen individually by four therapists working from dawn to dusk. Interpreters and practitioners experienced secondary trauma upon hearing of the horrors of the genocide that the Rwandans had endured and survived. In the course of treating the genocide survivors, as the practitioners and interpreters demonstrated the self-treatments, they essentially also simultaneously treated themselves for secondary trauma.

We used TFT on 50 orphaned adolescents who had been suffering with symptoms of PTSD. Scores on a PTSD checklist completed by caretakers and by the adolescents on a self-rated PTSD checklist significantly decreased after one TFT treatment. Participants exceeding the PTSD cutoffs decreased from 72% to 18% on the self-ratings. Dramatic reductions of PTSD symptoms as described were also reported in subsequent interviews with students and their caretakers. The initial improvements were maintained at the 1-year follow-up on both checklists.

Other children referred by their teachers for more severe problems were also seen individually. The rest of the children were seen in groups, some specific to their major problems, such as headaches and problems focusing. One child, whose entire family had been murdered, named each of the seven siblings he no longer had but resiliently stated with a genuine smile that now he had four hundred brothers and sisters. After treatment, several adolescents spontaneously asked about training to help other genocide survivors experience the same kind of relief from the day-mares and flashbacks they had experienced. The children's teachers were amazed at the transformation occurring right before their eyes. One teacher told me, "Their traumas have been set free, so their eyes are set on the future."

On our return visit a year later, on the anniversary of the genocide, we saw a transformation at the Rwandan Orphans Project. The children reported no flashbacks, nightmares, or rage, and said that they tapped themselves whenever they had problems. The teachers reported the difference TFT made, with the children concentrating better without posttraumatic stress symptoms, and many had passed their competitive exams to go on to the regular secondary schools. Teachers reported marked reduction in anxiety, inattentiveness, aggressive behaviors, social isolation, and depression. They also told us that the children had higher self-esteem and increased self-confidence, leading to more assertiveness, creativity, and accomplishments. We saw that the floors had been painstakingly cleaned by the children after we left and kept clean. The children also planted vegetables and fruit trees, and they had more than enough vegetables for their meals to have some surplus to market.

We returned to Rwanda for a total of 5 consecutive years for about a month each time. We worked with many adult survivors in these ensuing years and, more important, began training pastors, priests, teachers, counselors, nurses, psychologists, social workers, police officers, and community leaders so that they could continue helping others in their communities.

The transformative results were often immediately apparent as forlorn, depressed, and even vacant countenances sparkled with renewed energy, hope, faith, and release of 12 to 17 years of painful haunting and disturbing images from the horrors of their genocide experiences. Many had brutally lost many of their family and relatives. Many had escaped after being beaten, threatened with death, and subjected to atrocities. One had to dig her way out from under a pile of corpses. Another saw her spouse being stoned to death. Some had witnessed the brutal bashing of babies and the slaying of their children and loved ones. As the painful flashbacks receded into the past, feelings of rage, outrage, and revenge shifted to thoughts of peace, forgiving, reconciliation, and national reunification.

At the Izere Center in Byumba, Rwanda, under the leadership of Father Jean Marie Vianney Dushimiyimana and Father Augustin Nzabonimana, a TFT clinic has been established, and they are treating many in that community and the surrounding areas. The Rwandan TFT practitioners from the Izere Center have helped at the annual hundred-day mourning events in Rwanda and serve as a model for training and implementation of TFT counseling services. They are teaching TFT in their schools and prisons and helping thousands of trauma survivors to recovery and enhanced functioning and productivity.

(Note: Portions of the proceeds from this book will be going to the Izere Center and also to the Rwandan Orphans Project to help these dedicated Rwandans who are working so diligently to help with the healing of the wounds and pains of the large-scale trauma. Donations can be made through Nalaniikaleomana Foundation, a tax-exempt nonprofit organization for furthering humanitarian projects; www.nalaniikaleomanafoundation.com, nalaniikaleomanafoundation@nalaniikaleomanafoundation.com)

The following are letters and excerpts of reports from the Izere Center.

Dear Dr. Caroline,

In Rwanda, we had many problems caused by the genocide: suffering from trauma, guilt, anger, stress, disability or physical pain, and other psychological problems. Many people had neither hope nor ways to deal with these problems.

The TFT team treated many people and helped them, showing the power of TFT. They then trained 35 persons to become TFT therapists. Around 99% of treated people witnessed their healing. The following year, 33 more TFT therapists were trained.

We opened a TFT office at Izere Center where the therapists continue weekly helping a big number of people. Among our suffering clients, most of them were crying, hopeless, and after treatment they went home with joy and happiness. It was very encouraging, and hopeful for us to see our people coming out of their painful situations. We have one full-time and two part-time therapists regularly working, and others coming on community service events where we treat also people from different regions.

From 2009 to now, many thousands of people have been healed and we have many testimonies among them, there are those that are given by the local authorities, therapists, and clients. We are training the teachers at their schools in order to take care of their students. We are also training the prison staff and prisoners.

We sincerely appreciate and recognize from our heart, Dr. Caroline, the work of you and your colleagues.

Fr. Jean Marie Vianney Dushimiyimana (former chairperson of Izere Center)

Fr. Augustin Nzabonimana (chairperson of Izere Center)

Report from Father Augustin Nzabonimana:

A woman was brought in by others who had been successfully treated. She was fearful in the marketplace, in meetings, and even in church—she feared people would torture her or even kill her. After being treated with TFT, she now comes to church without fear, and goes to the market without problems. She brought her son who showed symptoms of grief and was silent, and never knew his father who was killed. The boy was not trusting of anyone. After treatment with TFT, the boy is talking, goes to school, and is behaving well.

Report from Adrienne Nahayo, psychologist:

A 34-year-old woman was in despair and felt desperate and hopeless. She had anxiety, guilt, depression, tried to commit suicide, felt mistrust, lacked self-confidence, and suffered from headaches and backaches. After TFT treatments, she believes she has value, and wants to start some business that can generate income.

A 22-year-old woman was extremely fearful. She was always afraid someone or something would surprise her from behind and hurt her or kill her. She had nightmares regularly. Her heart beat fast with fright and she ran from nothing. She ran from people she met on the street. She felt ashamed and lonely, could not sleep well, and had chronic headaches. After her TFT treatment, her fears have gone. She was so excited, as she had lived in fear for 13 years, since she was 9 years old.

Report from Father Jean Marie Vianney Dushimiyimana:

A 28-year-old very poor widow who is HIV-positive has five children. She was stressed, anguished, discouraged, and did not want to live with her children any more. She was seen for TFT treatments for 2 months, and she got stronger and felt better, started to feel love for her children and herself, and regained her inner peace.

Dear Dr. Caroline:

We recognize all your efforts and everything that you provided to Izere Center from 2009 to now; many thousands of people are and have been assisted by the therapists whom you trained. Our wishes are to see TFT growing, bearing many fruits in families, in services to youth, in service of widows, and in the whole Rwandan society which is still dealing with many problems caused by the war and the genocide of 1994.

I hope that your book will open the way for people of good will to help many people who are in need and many people in painful situations of war, conflict, poverty, and their consequences.

May God bless you all!

Bishop Servilien Nzakamwita, Bishop of Diocese of Byumba

We have witnessed how the tools of TFT can be readily taught and implemented to help empower communities devastated by large-scale trauma by aiding their recovery, healing, and renewed resilience. TFT has helped to shift feelings of rage, revenge, and fears to thoughts of reconciliation, unification, and peace as the flashbacks, nightmares, and haunting memories receded. Perspectives broadened as more positive images of the past and the future came into focus once the traumatic horrors faded from prominence.

This could provide a model for humanitarian efforts to help healing large-scale trauma. The Izere Center is demonstrating that process in Byumba, Rwanda. Hearing about the earlier work in Rwanda with TFT helping genocide survivors, Father Jean Marie Vianney (JMV) Dushimiyimana invited an ATFT Foundation team to help treat and train the people of their parish. Fathers JMV and Augustin selected representative community leaders from education, police, social service, business, clergy, orphanages, health services, government service, and so on to be trained. They treated people after they were trained under the supervision of visiting trainers, then continued to treat more people in the parish throughout the year, as well as following up with those that needed or desired further help. They continue the healing work in their places of employment or as volunteers or staff at the Izere Center. Father JMV and Father Augustin Nzabonimana shared their vision of expanding this model of training and treatment with TFT to other parishes and communities and countries in Africa affected by large-scale trauma. They and their team of therapists are participating in TFT community days and continue to work on promoting unity, peace, and reconciliation at Izere Center and in the region.

The Rwandans may well serve as a model for attaining recovery, instilling hope, and fostering reconciliation in our local communities in our struggles with homelessness and despair. After receiving advanced training in Hawaii, the Rwandans helped with training staff from several of the Hawaiian agencies serving the homeless and underserved and providing pro bono clinics we held at each site. As one agency leader noted, if the Rwandans can be so positive, resilient, and resourceful after the magnitude of what they have endured and overcome, surely we can make a positive difference with our comparatively smaller struggles.

We were all deeply inspired by the resilience, ability to forgive, and positive attitudes of the genocide survivors in Rwanda. Incredible examples of strength, caring, courage, gratitude, and love happened despite the horrific tragedies of their past. Their singular and collective eagerness to give back and help others was uplifting and heartwarming. They had tenaciously survived unspeakable horrors and daunting adversities, and they fervently expressed wishes to help other survivors. They expressed their eagerness to do whatever they could to help heal the wounds of traumas and prevent further atrocities, violence, and genocide and to promote peace and reconciliation in their country.

The following stories you are about to read are compelling, tragic, heartbreaking, hopeful, and inspiring. These stories truly reveal and epitomize the resilience of human beings.

LARGE-SCALE TRAUMA

20

Playful Memories

Be faithful in small things because it is in them that your strength lies.
—Mother Teresa

Fifteen-year-old Angelique was one of the few survivors from her village. At the time of the uprising, little Angelique was just 3 years old. Her family and other villagers had taken refuge inside the local church where they expected and hoped to be safe. However, at dusk, men bearing machetes stormed into the church and started the massacre. In the bedlam and chaos, her quick-thinking father yelled for her and others to run as fast as they could out of the church to escape. He told her to keep running and not look back for any reason. However, when she heard her father screaming in a frenzied, frantic way so unlike him, she turned to see what was happening. Under normal conditions, she was an obedient child, but she could not ignore his screams. As she looked back, she saw several men attacking her father with machetes. Since then, the flashbacks and nightmares of this gruesome attack had haunted her daily.

When I first met Angelique with an interpreter, she cried and her body shook as she shared her haunting memories with the interpreter and me. She appeared forlorn, with lowered head and stooped shoulders, and withdrawn, with a troubled expression in her face and eyes. She had trouble sleeping due to horrific nightmares and trouble concentrating in school because of the intrusive images and memories that kept flashing through her mind.

We were saddened and moved by her terrible traumas. We began the trauma algorithm, tapping through the layers of her intense memories. Her tears and unrelenting sadness and grief steadily transformed into smiles after several rounds of treatment in about half an hour. She joyfully reported fond memories of her father and family playing together, which she had not been able to remember before her TFT treatment. I noted that accessing fond memories again was a good sign of progress.

I then asked her to focus on what had happened inside the church, which brought a concerned look from my pastor interpreter, who had been pleased and relieved moments before, upon seeing the shift from crying to smiling. I explained that we wanted to continue to work through as much of her traumatic memories as we could to have as complete a treatment of these traumas as time and circumstances allowed. So I continued by asking her what feelings were coming up now when she thought about what happened in the church.

She began crying again as she recalled the other murders she had witnessed. She saw some of her other family members being brutally killed and worked through more traumatic memories with the trauma algorithm. She recalled that a boy, a few years older than she, grabbed her hand and helped her hide in the bushes once they were outside the church. From their hiding point, they witnessed the slaughter of their friends and neighbors who were attempting to flee from their pursuers. We continued with TFT trauma treatments until these memories also faded.

After multiple rounds of trauma treatments dealing with different facets of her traumatic memories, she started laughing aloud with glee as she recalled her father hiding sweet fruits in his pockets and sneaking them to her and her siblings when her mother was not looking. Her mother did not want the children to eat these fruits because she felt they were too sweet and would be bad for their teeth. Angelique's father and all the children loved to eat them, however, and he would find ways to get them past their mother.

This time when asked what else was coming up for her when she thought about the genocide, which she reported was now a distant and faded memory, she related other happy memories of her family. She saw them as they were before the genocide, rather than the freeze-frame of the horrors of their deaths, in which she had been stuck for 12 years. We ended her treatment for that day with a review of the trauma treatment sequence that she would repeat before bedtime and upon awakening with nightmares and asked her to return the following day.

When seen again the next day, Angelique reported no nightmares and no flashbacks of the traumatic memories. Instead, she was excited and elated about accessing fond memories of her early childhood, which the intrusive and overwhelming flashbacks had kept her from remembering. She was seen again the third day and again reported no nightmares and no flashbacks and was continuing to remember her loved ones as she knew them before the last horrendous moments of their lives. She was overjoyed to no longer have such painful images and recollections every time she thought of her family and to instead remember them as she wanted to cherish them—with fond memories of happier times.

Angelique then shared that she had prayed to be able to forgive those who killed her father and the other family members, relatives, friends, and neighbors. Previously, she had only been able to think words of forgiveness, but now she could actually feel the healing power of forgiveness and truly let go of the hurt and resentment of the past. She could not only say with conviction that she could forgive those who murdered her family, she could now also feel it from deep within her heart. She beamed with pride as she related how she had helped a younger child who had not yet had TFT treatment to tap her day-mares and nightmares away also. She wanted to learn more about how she could help the many others in the community who were still suffering from the trauma of the genocide. Angelique had transformed from haunted to happy, from withdrawn to reaching out to help others, and from forlorn and depressed to enthusiastic and optimistic about her life.

TFT Treatments for Angelique

Trauma
Eyebrow Under eye Under nose Under collarbone 9 Gamut process Repeat acupoint sequence Reversal: side of hand

Trauma with Grief, Sadness, and Depression
Eyebrow Under eye Under nose Under collarbone Gamut spot Under collarbone 9 Gamut process Repeat acupoint sequence Reversal: side of hand

21
Giving Back

As we express our gratitude, we must never forget that the highest
appreciation is not to utter words, but to live by them.

—John F. Kennedy

The haunting memories and flashbacks that plagued survivors during their waking hours and disturbed their sleep in turbulent nightmares were exacerbated by questions about why their loved ones, family, friends, and neighbors perished and they survived. Survivor guilt may be one of the contributing factors in the common reaction to relief of one's pain and suffering: wanting to give back and contribute to helping others.

A stately senior gentleman, Alphonse was haunted daily by the gruesome flashbacks and nightmares of being forced to witness his wife and children being murdered right in front of him. Then he was viciously hacked with machetes four times on his head and neck. Miraculously, he survived but had not functioned normally since these traumatic events, suffering physical problems, depressive grief, and survivor's guilt.

We used TFT on his oppressive traumas, grief, and pain that felt like a vise gripping him. As he tapped through multiple layers of these horrors, his agonized face and intense posture increasingly relaxed into release and peace. The sharp, intrusive images faded into the distance, losing intensity, vividness of color, and excruciating detail. He felt a sense of inner calm and peace that he had not known since the genocide. He breathed a deep sigh of relief as he was able to expand his focus and recollect fond memories of his beloved wife and lively children.

Alphonse returned the next day excited and pleased that he'd had a deep and restful sleep for the first time in 12 agonizing years. He described how his flashbacks during the waking hours were gone. His nightmares, which he had been experiencing almost every night, were previously so disturbing that he had dreaded bedtime. He expressed gratitude at having both the flashbacks and nightmares cease their relentless replays of the most horrendous and despicable memories imaginable. He now asked for help with the dizziness and falling that had begun after the genocide.

He explained that the dizziness made him lose his balance and fall, which was why he had red dirt all over his clothing. I assumed he had a neurological problem from the injuries he sustained during the genocide. Medical treatment had not been physically and financially accessible to him. With the diagnostic level of TFT, a treatment protocol was determined to try to help lower his distress. To the surprise of the interpreter and me, he reported that the dizziness was gone after the treatment. I assumed it must be a placebo effect and ran after him to be sure that he took his cane with him as he left. Reflecting upon it later, I thought perhaps the somatic residuals of the traumatic events locked in the freeze-frames of his memory were released in some way. Physical symptoms can remit upon treatment of the underlying trauma, which the body appears to be able to store in somatic memories.

The next day, Alphonse came back to thank us for his newfound health with the treatment of his traumas and debilitating symptoms. He told his fellow villagers about his treatments, and when he walked back to the orphanage to give thanks, over two dozen villagers followed him. They wanted to have this same treatment too. As we had about four hundred orphans to treat, we let them know we would treat those we could, but that we would be training the pastors, teachers, and community leaders with TFT so that they could help others in the Rwandan community with their traumas.

On Easter Sunday, Alphonse came to the church service at the orphanage. At the end of the service, he stood up to share that he was now well; he no longer had dizziness, flashbacks, and nightmares. He wanted to give back to the orphanage for inviting the TFT treatment team to Rwanda and giving him the opportunity to experience the healing of his genocide traumas and resulting symptoms. He announced his desire to open his humble home to take in three or four orphans. Now that he had his life and full functioning back, he wanted to help others. He was seeking a way of giving back and finding a purpose for his survival through doing what he could to help others in his community.

TFT Treatments for Alphonse

Trauma with Grief and Emotional Pain
Eyebrow Under eye Under arm Under collarbone Gamut spot Under collarbone Eyebrow Under collarbone 9 Gamut process Repeat acupoint sequence Reversal: side of hand, under nose
Psychological Reversal, Trauma, Pain, Anger, Rage, and Survivor Guilt
Side of hand Eyebrow Under eye Under arm Under collarbone Gamut spot Under collarbone Tiny finger Outside edge of eye Index finger Under collarbone 9 Gamut process Repeat acupoint sequence Reversal: under nose

22

Somersaulting with Joy

Wealth, like happiness, is never attained when sought after directly. It comes as a by-product of providing a useful service.

—Henry Ford

Some of the orphaned children we worked with did not necessarily remember specific details of the massacre, being under 5 years old at the time. Yet as we know from studies and trials, children who witness horrific acts of violence are traumatized at deep levels. The effects of their traumas show up in the form of anger, insomnia, nightmares, and more. One such example was a 13-year-old boy named Jeremiah whose life was quite restricted by his fears.

Jeremiah told us that he was terrified of the dark and would sit on his bed when the sun went down. He would shake and be too scared to move without knowing exactly why he was so frightened. His fears would start at dusk, and he would freeze into a withdrawn position once the sun went down. As there was no electricity and battery-generated power was only used for special events, the orphanage was dark once the sun set. Jeremiah did not remember any details of the genocide except that he has always been fearful of the dark. Other children told him that they did not like the darkness either, as some of their traumatic memories arose at night.

Jeremiah's immediate symptoms included heart palpitations, sweaty palms, clenched fists, tense shoulders, and rounded back. It was almost like he was curling up to protect himself from an unknown assailant. As Jeremiah tapped on the treatment meridian acupoints for trauma, his posture straightened, his fists relaxed, his shoulders dropped, and he reported that his heart had stopped knocking on his chest. He grinned from ear to ear and proudly announced that he was not afraid of the dark anymore. He said he could not wait until dusk came because he wanted to play with the other children at night, as he had longed to do for as many years as he could remember.

The next day, he excitedly greeted our bus and bubbled over with joy. He had played with the other children, shooting marbles and playing games from after dusk until bedtime. He gave us big grins, high fives, and a heartfelt "murakoze cyane cyane" (thank you very much)!

After we had worked with other children that day, he came up as we were getting ready to leave and asked if he could show how happy he was. I wasn't sure what he meant by that, as he indicated he wanted to go outdoors to show his joy at getting his night back. Jeremiah then ran a short distance and did a somersault of joy into the air, with a huge grin.

The day we were leaving Rwanda, he came up to us with eyes full of tears as he said "thank you" over and over. He wished us a safe journey and hoped we would come back to visit again someday. Jeremiah's only possessions were his few sets of clothes, his one pair of slippers, his thin well-worn blanket, and three well-used and slightly cracked marbles. He seemed to be trying to open my hand as we shook hands good-bye.

I shook his hand, as I couldn't understand the rest of what he was saying in his native Kinyarwanda. He was one of the many students who did not speak or understand any French or English. One of the teachers came by and explained that Jeremiah wanted to give me a token of appreciation for helping him overcome his fear of the dark. He wanted to share one of his three precious marbles as a gift of appreciation. I was very moved by his generosity and asked him to pose for a photo with his marbles, as a treasured photo of his appreciation.

TFT Treatments for Jeremiah

Psychological Reversal with Trauma-Related Phobia
Side of hand Eyebrow Under eye Under arm Under collarbone 9 Gamut process Repeat acupoint sequence Reversal: under nose

23

Freedom at Last

Faith is taking the first step even when you don't see the whole staircase.
—Martin Luther King Jr.

Sometimes severe posttraumatic stress can present in ways that may look like irrational behaviors or even delusional thinking, violent acting out or self-harm behaviors, severe withdrawal, or wild mood swings. One of the Rwandan therapists sought help for "someone who could not be helped." He explained to me that the older woman was not even able to look at him, could not talk coherently, seemed to be in her own world, yelled loudly, and thrashed about as if she would either strike out or run away at any moment. This older woman, Elizabeth, also heard voices. He explained that she would yell about the people coming to kill her and her children. It was apparent that in her highly agitated state, she was reliving the traumas and horrors of the genocide as if it were occurring right in the moment.

When we met Elizabeth, she was unable to focus, and she had a vacant, frightened look. Then, as the therapist talked to this seemingly unresponsive woman about helping with her traumatic memories of the genocide, she started gritting her teeth and began looking extremely agitated. Elizabeth looked around at the voices she was hearing that were threatening to kill her and her family and talked back to them while rolling her eyes. She then began waving her arms, stamping her feet on the ground, and tipping backward on the bench where she was sitting.

One of the other Rwandan therapists walked over from where he had been working with another survivor to offer support and help since Elizabeth was screaming and flailing around. She was oblivious to his presence as well as to our presence right in front of her. At that point, she spat and stood up as if she was going to bolt out into the surrounding fields. The therapist asked Elizabeth's permission to help. When she did not object, he started tapping on the side of her hand. He initiated the tapping as she stood frozen, not sure what to do. He then proceeded with the trauma algorithm, and she sat back down. She was calmer, and her yelling stopped. The psychological reversal treatment and initiation of the trauma algorithm helped her become more grounded in the here and now. Elizabeth shook her head as she started to look directly and intently at the Rwandan therapist and me as if actually seeing us for the first time. She looked about fearfully, trembled, and gritted her teeth. She was calmer, but we had a ways to go.

The Rwandan therapist then did a TFT diagnostic assessment after she indicated it was all right to touch her wrist, and he continued treatment, using the diagnostic treatment points. Her agitation subsided even more. Elizabeth remained focused, her body visibly relaxed, and the light went back on in her eyes. The gritted teeth relaxed into a broad smile of release and relief. The voices disappeared, and she maintained good eye contact, being fully present. She no longer went in and out of dissociation and was not responding to compelling internal experiences.

The other therapist went back to treat the survivor with whom he had been working, with a nod and smile as he saw that Elizabeth had been calmed down and was no longer posing any threat.

Her only fear at the end of treatment, when her SUD level went from 10 plus (estimate obtained after her treatment) to 0, was that her disturbing and distressing symptoms might return. Even though she could not read, we gave her a written treatment protocol in Kinyarwanda. Elizabeth lived with the surviving seven of her 13 children and a few of them could read, so they could help her. She also was informed of the ongoing TFT services that would be available twice a week at the Izere Center. She stated with amazement that it was as if she had been lost and now found her way home. She stated that it was now quiet in her head without the voices and painful flashbacks. She no longer felt she was cursed, and the stabbing pains in her chest and stomach had disappeared. Elated, she expressed her joy and gratitude for this release and relief.

The Rwandan therapist was incredulous at the transformation he'd seen. He had not thought anything like that would be possible with TFT. He shared his experience with the other therapists at the debriefing. It illuminated how the traumatic flashbacks of the genocide could manifest in such intense ways, how people could be extremely agitated when coming out of the dissociated states, and how they could become grounded and work through such severe states with TFT.

TFT Treatments for Elizabeth

Psychological Reversal
Side of hand
Trauma
Eyebrow Under eye Under arm Under collarbone

The diagnostically determined sequence was essentially psychological reversal plus trauma with anger, rage, pain, and guilt algorithms.

Side of hand
Eyebrow
Under eye
Under arm
Under collarbone
Tiny finger
Outside edge of eye
Gamut spot
Under collarbone
Index finger
Under collarbone

9 Gamut process
Repeat acupoint sequence
Reversals: under nose

Afterword:
Steps We Can All Take Toward Healing

What a different world this could become if we all had the skills to tap our maladies into manageable challenges, to heal our traumas and pains, to overcome adversities, and to develop more resilience and grow in gratitude. It would be a world with an abundance of health and energy to live life more fully and robustly, to place more emphases on creativity and enjoyment of healthy joys, to challenge ourselves to be the best we can be in wherever our talents and interests abound, and to expend our energies and resources on acts of kindness and charity.

Prevention of illness and the promotion of wellness would be the mainstays of our health care system. We would all be learning skills to enhance our health and well-being, rather than just relying on pills. We could reduce our health care treatment costs for illnesses that can be averted, prevented, or mitigated—including diabetes, heart disease, and cancer—and have more resources to utilize in education and programs for understanding lifestyle practices that enhance our nutritional well-being, physical movement optimization, psychological health, and spirituality. We could embrace and integrate all the wellness practices that move us in this healthier living direction.

We are not doomed by our genetics or our history. We have choices in what we do in the present and future, and we can use the knowledge and wisdom we've gained from the past, including learning from mistakes, which we all make in our lives. Forgiving ourselves and others can be part of the healing journey to living more peaceful, healthy, harmonious, and productive lives.

We can transform from focusing on our ills, grievances, annoyances, peeves, pains, hurts, resentments, misfortunes, and tragedies and reliving them endlessly or numbing out to addressing them and moving onward. We don't have to be stuck in depression, victimization, hate, anger, hurt, and resentment. We can transcend our traumas and physical and emotional pains to live with grace and gratitude in a life of joy, with the blessings that come with being able to be of help and service to others as well as ourselves.

We can all take steps toward taking better control of our own body, mind, and spirit. Practical steps each of us can choose include:

a) Focus on what you have to be grateful for each day.

b) Take active and proactive steps to change and transform what keeps you in negative states.

c) Find a practitioner of Energy Psychology.

d) Take a class in energy healing.

e) Read more (see the resource list in Appendix H).

f) Take action today by starting to do these steps to make a difference in your life!

We can optimize our healing and growth, and utilize tapping (or mental refocusing) as a way to enhance health and harmony. We can choose to take the path of posttraumatic growth to resilience, gratitude, and attainment of our highest potential. We can contribute to making ourselves the best that we can be, and to making our world a little healthier and better place to live. We can be the change we want to see in the world.

APPENDICES

Appendix A:
Location of the Treatment
Acupoints

Eyebrow:	At the start of the eyebrow, above the bridge of the nose.
Under eye:	In line with the center of the eye, on the rim of the eye socket bone (alternative if unable to tap on the face: inner side of second toe).
Outer eye:	About 3/4 inch out horizontally from the outer edge of the eye, on the edge of the eye socket.
Under nose:	Under nose and above the upper lip.
Under lip:	Below the lower lip, in the middle of the chin.
Under arm:	On the side of the body, about 4 inches or one palm width under the armpit.
Under collarbone:	From between the two collarbone notches at the V of the neck down an inch and over an inch on either side.
Gamut spot:	On the back of the hand, in the indentation between the tiny finger and the ring finger starting about 1/2 inch down on the back of the hand—use three fingers to tap in that valley.

Tiny finger:	On the side of the nail on the thumb side.
Index finger:	On the side of the nail on the thumb side.
Middle finger:	On the side of the nail on the thumb side.
Side of hand:	On the blade of the open hand where the line crossing the palm ends and forms a creased bump if the hand is closed; also called the PR (Psychological Reversal) point or Karate Chop point.
Tender spot:	Down an inch from between the two collarbone notches at the V of the neck and horizontally to the left about 3 or more inches to the spot that is tender to touch (lymphatic drainage).

Treatment Points

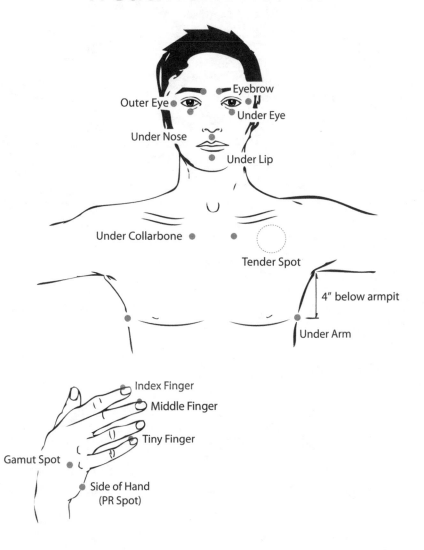

Eyebrow

Outer Eye

Under Eye

Under Nose

Under Lip

Under Collarbone

Tender Spot

4" below armpit

Under Arm

Index Finger

Middle Finger

Tiny Finger

Gamut Spot

Side of Hand
(PR Spot)

Appendix B:
TFT Steps

TFT treatment algorithms generally have the same pattern:

Acupoint sequence (specific for the thought field).

9 Gamut process:

1. Close eyes.

2. Open eyes.

3. Keep head still and look down to one side with eyes.

4. Keep head still and look down to other side with eyes.

5. Roll eyes around in a circle in one direction.*

6. Roll eyes around in a circle in the opposite direction.

7. Hum different notes.

8. Count to five.

9. Hum different notes.

Acupoint sequence (repeat previous acupoint sequence).

---

* Skipped or modified if there is retinal detachment or other issues that would entail discomfort with eye rolls.

When the distress is down to 0 or as low as the person can or chooses to attain, the treatment is complete. A floor-to-ceiling eye roll can be done for further relaxation and for ending the treatment: While tapping on the Gamut spot and keeping the head level, look down to the floor and slowly let the eyes move upward toward the ceiling and then relax to normal eye level.

If further distress remains, reversals can be used, followed by another round of the treatment sequence. The sequence is called a holon and is sometimes referred to as a 9 Gamut sandwich because there are acupoint sequences on both ends with the 9 Gamut process in the middle. For example, the anger algorithm would be:

Under eye

Under arm

Under collarbone

9 Gamut process

Under eye

Under arm

Under collarbone

If the SUD level has gone to 0, treatment would end here or could optionally be concluded with the floor-to-ceiling eye roll.

If the SUD level is still high, the reversals would be used, followed by the holon (9 Gamut sandwich) until the SUD rating drops to the lowest level attainable.

Reversals:

Side of hand, repeat the holon

Tender spot, repeat the holon

Index finger, repeat the holon

Under nose, repeat the holon

Collarbone breathing can also be used when the treatment is progressing very slowly (see Appendix D). If the distress is not dropping even with two reversals, a different algorithm or combination may be needed, or an individually diagnosed acupoint sequence. Generally, one would discontinue and reassess if no progress is being made.

Appendix C:
Commonly Used Algorithms

Acupoints are generally tapped about 5 to 10 times (without counting), continuing longer if noticing changes until reaction stabilizes. Side of hand tends to be longer, about 10 to 15 times. Gamut spot is about 30 to 50 times, about a half minute.

The algorithm acupoints are followed by the 9 Gamut process (see Appendix B), followed by a repeat of the same acupoints. Reversals are used if needed, followed by a repetition of the acupoints, 9 Gamut process, acupoints.

Common TFT Treatment Algorithms

Addictive Craving	Under eye, under arm, under collarbone
Anger	Tiny finger, under collarbone
Anxiety	Under eye, under arm, under collarbone
Clumsiness	Collarbone breathing
Depression	Gamut spot, under collarbone
Embarrassment	Under nose
Grief	Gamut spot, under collarbone; Eyebrow, under collarbone
Guilt	Index finger, under collarbone

Inhalant Reaction	Middle finger, under arm, under collarbone
Low Self-Esteem	Side of hand, index finger, eyebrow, under eye, under arm, under collarbone, under eye, under collarbone, under nose, under lip
Nasal Congestion	Side of hand, under nose, middle finger, under arm, under collarbone
Negativity	Side of hand
Obsessive Thoughts	Under collarbone, under eye, under collarbone
Pain	Gamut spot, under collarbone
Panic Attacks	Eyebrow, under eye, under arm, under collarbone
Phobia	Under eye, under arm, under collarbone
Phobia—Turbulence, Claustrophobia, Spiders	Under arm, under eye, under collarbone
Rage	Outer eye, under collarbone
Rejection, Love Pain	Eyebrow, under collarbone
Shame	Under lip
Stress	Side of hand, under eye, under arm, under collarbone
Trauma	Eyebrow, under eye, under arm, under collarbone

Appendix D:
Collarbone Breathing

Collarbone breathing is used to help increase focus and concentration. It can also help with coordination and balance.

Indications for collarbone breathing are:

- TFT treatment is moving very slowly or stalling.
- Psychological reversals are not working or not holding well.
- Awkwardness and poor coordination.
- Reversing actions, concepts, directions.
- Drowsiness when reading.
- Attention deficits.
- Too easily distracted.

Collarbone Breathing Procedure

Two activities are done simultaneously:

- Breathing sequence.
- Tapping in different positions and locations.

Breathing Sequence

1. Breathe normally.
2. Take a full breath through your nose from your diaphragm and hold it.
3. Let half of the breath out.

4. Let all the breath out.

5. Take a half breath in from your diaphragm and hold it.

6. Release and breathe normally.

Tapping Positions and Locations

1. Place two fingertips on one of the collarbone points (down an inch, over an inch from between the collarbone notches).

2. Tap the Gamut spot on the back of that hand while doing the breathing sequence (about five taps per breathing position).

3. Move the two fingertips to the other collarbone point and repeat the breathing sequence.

4. Fold the fingers of the same hand over the thumb and touch the collarbone point with your knuckles while doing the breathing sequence.

5. Move the knuckles under the other collarbone and repeat the breathing sequence.

6. Then repeat the hand positions with the other hand, touching one of the collarbone points while tapping on the Gamut spot of this other hand and doing the breathing positions.

Appendix E:
Peak Performance

Peak performance enhances your confidence level once you have treated the barriers that impede your path to performing optimally in whatever you are working on. For example, you could enhance: public speaking, performing in the zone in specific sports, playing music, singing, asking for what you need, setting clear boundaries, and handling challenges calmly.

You need to start with a level of confidence of at least 2 on a 0 to 10 scale. If your confidence falls below that, there are still some barriers to work on or specific skills to build first. For example, I can work on my running as I have some experience and strength training with it, but I can't work on specific golf swings until I learn them well enough to have body memory about the desired movements, posture, and balance.

Use all your sensory modalities to visualize yourself doing the activity in detail—with your facial expression, how you're dressed, body posture, and how you're moving—and feel that physically in your body. Bring in all the sounds that go with that activity and any tastes and smells that are relevant. You can do this with your eyes open or closed.

When you have that clearly in mind, then tap:

Under arm

Under collarbone

9 Gamut process

    1. Close eyes.

    2. Open eyes.

    3. Keep head still and look down to one side with eyes.

    4. Keep head still and look down to other side with eyes.

    5. Roll eyes around in a circle in one direction.

    6. Roll eyes around in a circle in the opposite direction.

    7. Hum different notes.

    8. Count to five.

    9. Hum different notes.

Repeat visualizing your performance in detail, feeling it kinesthetically in your body, hearing the sounds that go with it, and including tastes and smells if appropriate.

When you have that clearly in mind, then tap:

Under arm

Under collarbone

If you need to enhance your confidence level further, you can use psychological reversal treatments, followed by repeating the previous sequence of visualization, acupoints, 9 Gamut, visualization, acupoints.

Reversals: Side of hand, tender spot, under nose.

Appendix F:
Pulse Testing for Individual Energy Sensitivities

Arthur F. Coca, MD, developed pulse testing as a method for identifying substances to which your body is sensitive (Coca, 1994). To do this test, take your pulse for 1 full minute while you are sitting, then for 1 full minute in a standing position. If your standing pulse minus your sitting pulse equals 10 or more, this may be an indication of individualized energy sensitivity. Also, a resting pulse count of 80 and above, in the absence of a medical or physical explanation, suggests it would be useful to collect information that might help identify the causes.

Energy Toxin Pulse Testing Daily Log

Take a full-minute pulse:

1. Upon waking in the morning or before getting out of bed.

2. Before each meal.

3. After each meal (30, 60, or 90 minutes later).

4. After any inhalant exposure.

5. Before going to bed at night.

If pulse rate is in the 80s and above, write down everything inhaled or ingested (eaten or drunk) prior to the elevation.

Detective work can help to identify what your body is sensitive to at this particular time. Stress, toxic exposure, and other factors can raise the sensitivity and reactivity. Eliminating the energy toxin for 2 months could give the body an opportunity to function more efficiently and healthfully.

Dr. Doris Rapp, in her work with toxic chemicals in our daily environments, conceptualized the full barrel effect. If we have exposure or ingestion of just one or two things to which we are sensitive, we may not exhibit symptoms, but when the effects of stress, sleep deprivation, and multiple exposures or ingested substances get us to the top of our barrel, we may become ill or symptomatic.

Once we discover through pulse logs, energy tests, or other means of self-research about our sensitivities, we can avoid those items that are not essential, and lower what we carry around in our barrel. When we are under stress, or have indulged in something to which we have had reactions, we can aid our health and well-being by being even more diligent in avoiding substances that may lower our immune function and make us ill or symptomatic.

Appendix G:
Summary of Kaiser HMO Applications

The following summarizes a Kaiser HMO's program evaluation of different applications of TFT.

Dx or Sx	N	Mean (Range) SUD-Pre	Mean (Range) SUD-Post	Mean SUD Diff	SD	T
Acute Stress	13	7.69 (5-10)	1.19 (0-6)	6.50	2.25	10.44*
Adjustment Disorder with Anxiety	27	7.65 (4-10)	1.00 (0-4)	6.65	2.46	14.02*
Adjustment Disorder with Anxiety/ Depression	8	7.37 (3-10)	1.37 (0-5)	6.00	2.62	6.48*
Adjustment Disorder with Depression	12	6.50 (3-10)	0.83 (0-7)	5.67	2.35	8.36*
Alcohol Cravings+	5	6.80 (5-10)	0.40 (0-2)	6.40	2.51	5.70**
Anger	162	8.18 (2.5-10)	1.02 (0-9)	7.16	2.42	37.67*
Anxiety	216	7.54 (3-10)	0.86 (0-6)	6.68	2.25	43.53*
Anxiety Due to Medical Condition	78	7.83 (3-10)	1.46 (0-6.5)	6.38	2.72	20.69*
Bereavement	16	7.00 (3-10)	1.41 (0-5)	5.59	2.25	9.97*
Chronic Pain	234	6.82 (1-10)	2.24 (0-9)	4.58	2.55	27.42*
Depression	106	7.35 (2.5-10)	1.59 (0-8)	5.76	2.55	23.26*
Fatigue	47	7.23 (3-10)	1.91 (0-8)	5.32	2.37	15.39*
Major Depressive Disorder	6	8.50 (7-10)	2.50 (0-7)	6.00	2.45	6.00**

Maladaptive Food+ Cravings	142	8.14 (3-10)	0.67 (0-9)	7.47	2.18	40.84*
Nausea	15	6.40 (2-10)	0.67 (0-5)	5.73	2.63	8.44*
Neurodermatitis	8	6.50 (4-10)	0.0 (0)	6.50	2.73	6.75*
Nicotine Cravings+	29	7.45 (4-10)	0.28 (0-4)	7.17	2.28	16.91*
Obsessive Traits	29	8.06 (3-10)	1.17 (0-5)	6.89	2.26	16.42*
OCD	9	8.39 (7-10)	1.61 (0-6)	6.78	2.40	8.47*
OCPD	12	6.67 (3-10)	0.83 (0-3)	5.83	2.72	7.42*
Panic Disorder w/o Agoraphobia	29	7.76 (4-10)	1.50 (0-5)	6.26	2.45	13.75*
Parent-Child Stress	12	8.13 (4-10)	1.75 (0-5)	6.37	2.51	8.81*
Partner Relation Stress	16	7.81 (3-10)	1.69 (0-7)	6.12	2.69	9.12*
PTSD	142	8.71 (1-10)	1.22 (0-8)	7.49	2.27	39.37*
Relationship Stress	55	7.71 (3-10)	0.84 (0-5)	6.87	2.32	21.93*
Social Phobia	22	8.41 (3-10)	1.07 (0-6)	7.34	2.22	15.50*
Specific Phobia	49	8.15 (3-10)	1.45 (0-7)	6.66	2.41	19.39*
Tremor	7	5.86 (4-10)	1.50 (0-3.5)	4.36	2.84	4.06**
Trichotillomania	11	7.36 (4-10)	0.91 (0-5)	6.45	2.11	10.12*
Type A/Histrionic Traits	10	8.70 (5-10)	2.95 (0-9.5)	5.75	3.54	5.14*
Work Stress	67	7.66 (4-10)	1.45 (0-8)	6.21	2.47	20.58*

+Subjective level of urge (LOU) was substituted for SUD with cravings

*p < 0.001

**p < 0.01

Source: Sakai, C., Paperny, D., Mathews, M., Tanida, G., Boyd, G., Simons, A., Yamamoto, C., Mau, C., & Nutter, L. (2001). Thought Field Therapy clinical applications: Utilization in an HMO in behavioral medicine and behavioral health services. *Journal of Clinical Psychology, 57*(10), 1215–1227.

Appendix H:
Energy Psychology Resources

For severe symptoms and clinical conditions, consult with a licensed psychologist, social worker, or other licensed mental health practitioner with expertise in treating those conditions or disorders. Many licensed clinicians have been trained in TFT, Clinical EFT, and/or the Association for Comprehensive Energy Psychology (ACEP) Comprehensive Energy Psychology Certification.

Websites

Practitioners and trainers in your area can be located through the following websites:

www.tftcenter.com

www.rogercallahan.com (TFT)

www.eftuniverse.com (Clinical EFT)

www.energypsych.org (ACEP)

Books

Bray, R. (2009). *No open wounds—Heal traumatic stress NOW: Complete recovery with Thought Field Therapy*. Los Gatos, CA: Robertson Publishing.

Callahan, R. J. (1985). *Five minute phobia cure*. Wilmington, DE: Enterprise.

Callahan, R. J., & Trubo, R. (2001). *Tapping the healer within*. New York, NY: McGraw-Hill.

Church, D., & Marohn, S. (Eds.). (2013). *Clinical EFT handbook: A definitive resource for practitioners, scholars, clinicians, and researchers*. Fulton, CA: Energy Psychology Press.

Coca, A. F. (1994). *The pulse test: The secret of building your basic health* (Rev. ed.). New York, NY: Barricade Books.

Connolly, S. M. (2004). *Thought Field Therapy: Clinical applications integrating TFT in psychotherapy*. Sedona, AZ: George Tyrrell Press.

Feinstein, D. (2004). *Energy psychology interactuve: Rapid techniques for lasting change*. Ashland, OR: Innersource.

Feinstein, D., Eden, D., & Craig, G. (2005). *The Promise of Energy Psychology: Revolutionary tools for dramatic personal change*. New York, NY: Penguin.

Articles

Connolly, S. M., Roe-Sepowitz, D., & Sakai, C. E. (2013). Utilizing community resources to treat PTSD: A randomized controlled study using Thought Field Therapy. *African Journal of Traumatic Stress, 3*(1), 24–32.

Connolly, S. M., & Sakai. C. E. (2011). Brief trauma intervention with Rwandan genocide survivors using Thought Field Therapy. *International Journal of Emergency Mental Health, 13*(3), 161–172.

Feinstein, D. (2012). Acupoint stimulation in treating psychological disorders: Evidence of efficacy. *Review of General Psychology, 16*, 364–380. doi:10.1037/a0028602

Sakai, C. S., Connolly, S. M., & Oas, P. (2010). Treatment of PTSD in Rwandan child genocide survivors using thought field therapy. *International Journal of Emergency Mental Health, 12*, 41–49. PMID:20828089

Sakai, C., Paperny, D., Mathews, M., Tanida, G., Boyd, G., Simons, A., Yamamoto, C., Mau, C., & Nutter, L. (2001). Thought Field

Therapy clinical applications: Utilization in an HMO in behavioral medicine and behavioral health services. *Journal of Clinical Psychology, 57*(10), 1215–1227.

Wylie, M. S. (1996). Researching PTSD: Going for the cure. *Family Therapy Networker,* July–August, 21–37.

Essential References for EP Practitioners

Feinstein, D., & Eden, D. (2011). *Ethics handbook for energy healing practitioners.* Fulton, CA: Energy Psychology Press.

Hover-Kramer, D. (2011). *Creating healing relationships: Professional standards for energy therapy practitioners.* Santa Rosa, CA: Energy Psychology Press.

References

Callahan, R. J. (1985). *Five minute phobia cure*. Wilmington, DE: Enterprise.

Callahan, R. J., & Trubo, R. (2001). *Tapping the healer within*. New York, NY: McGraw-Hill.

Cherkin, D. C., Sherman, K. J., Avins, A. L., Erro, J. H., Ichikawa, L., Barlow, W. E.,...Deyo, R. A. (2009, May 11). A randomized trial comparing acupuncture, simulated acupuncture, and usual care for chronic low back pain. *Archives of Internal Medicine, 169*(9), 858–866. doi:10.1001/archinternmed.2009.65

Church, D., & Marohn, S. (Eds.). (2013). *Clinical EFT handbook: A definitive resource for practitioners, scholars, clinicians, and researchers*. Fulton, CA: Energy Psychology Press.

Church, D., Yount, G., & Brooks, A. J. (2012). The effect of emotional freedom techniques on stress biochemistry: A randomized controlled trial. *Journal of Nervous and Mental Disease, 200*(10), 891–896. doi:10.1097/NMD.0b013e31826b9fc1

Coca, A. F. (1994). *The pulse test: The secret of building your basic health* (Rev. ed.). New York, NY: Barricade Books.

Connolly, S. M. (2004). *Thought Field Therapy: Clinical applications integrating TFT in psychotherapy*. Sedona, AZ: George Tyrrell Press.

Connolly, S. M., Roe-Sepowitz, D., & Sakai, C. E. (2013). Utilizing community resources to treat PTSD: A randomized controlled study using Thought Field Therapy. *African Journal of Traumatic Stress, 3*(1), 24–32.

Connolly, S. M., & Sakai. C. E. (2011). Brief trauma intervention with Rwandan genocide survivors using Thought Field Therapy. *International Journal of Emergency Mental Health, 13*(3), 161–172.

Diepold, J. H., Britt, V., & Bender, S. S. (2004). *Evolving Thought Field Therapy: The clinician's handbook of diagnosis, treatment, and theory.* New York, NY: W. W. Norton.

Fang, J., Jin, Z., Wang, Y., Li, K., Kong, J., Nixon, E. E.,...Hui, K. K.-S. (2009). The salient characteristics of the central effects of acupuncture needling: Limbic-paralimbic-neocortical network modulation. *Human Brain Mapping, 30,* 1196–1206. doi:10.1002/hbm.20583.

Feinstein, D. (2008). Energy psychology: A review of the preliminary evidence. *Psychotherapy: Theory, Research, Practice, Training, 45*(2), 199–213.

Feinstein, D. (2010). Rapid treatment of PTSD: Why psychological exposure with acupoint tapping may be effective. *Psychotherapy: Theory, Research, Practice, Training, 47,* 385–402. doi:10.1037/a0021171

Feinstein, D. (2012). Acupoint stimulation in treating psychological disorders: Evidence of efficacy. *Review of General Psychology, 16,* 364–380. doi:10.1037/a0028602

Folkes, C. E. (2002). Thought Field Therapy and trauma recovery. *International Journal of Emergency Mental Health, 4*(2), 99–103.

Georgopoulos, A. P., Tan, H.-R. M., Lewis, S. M., Leuthold, A. C., Winskowski, A. M., Lynch, J. K., & Engdahl, B. (2010). The synchronous neural interactions test as a functional neuromarker for posttraumatic stress disorder (PTSD): A robust classification method based on the bootstrap. *Journal of Neural Engineering, 7*(1), 16011. doi:10.1088/1741-2560/7/1/016011

Hui, K. K., Liu, J., Makris, N, Gollub, R. L., Chen, A. J., Moore, C. I.,... Kwong, K. K. (2000). Acupuncture modulates the limbic system and subcortical gray structures of the human brain: Evidence from fMRI studies in normal subjects. *Human Brain Mapping, 9*(1), 13–25.

Johnson, C., Shala, M., Sejdijaj, X., Odell, R., & Dabishevci, K. 2001. Thought Field Therapy: Soothing the bad moments of Kosovo. *Journal of Clinical Psychology, 57*(10), 1237–1240.

Lambrou, P. T., Pratt, G. J., & Chevalier, G. (2003). Physiological and psychological effects of a mind/body therapy on claustrophobia. *Subtle Energies and Energy Medicine, 14*, 239–251.

Rapp, D. J. (1991). *Is this your child? Discovering and treating unrecognized allergies in children and adults.* New York, NY: Quill/William Morrow.

Rapp, D. J. (1996). *Is this your child's world? How you can fix the schools and homes that are making your children sick.* New York, NY: Bantam Books.

Sakai, C. S., Connolly, S. M., & Oas, P. (2010). Treatment of PTSD in Rwandan child genocide survivors using thought field therapy. *International Journal of Emergency Mental Health, 12*, 41–49. PMID:20828089

Sakai, C., Paperny, D., Mathews, M., Tanida, G., Boyd, G., Simons, A., Yamamoto, C., Mau, C., & Nutter, L. (2001). Thought Field Therapy clinical applications: Utilization in an HMO in behavioral medicine and behavioral health services. *Journal of Clinical Psychology, 57*(10), 1215–1227.

Schoninger, B., & Hartung, J. (2010). Changes on self-report measures of public speaking anxiety following treatment with Thought Field Therapy. *Energy Psychology: Theory, Research, and Treatment, 2*(1), 13–26. doi:10.9769.EPJ.2010.2.1.BS

Wolpe, J. (1958). *Psychotherapy by reciprocal inhibition.* Stanford, CA: Stanford University Press.

About the Author

Photo by Dwight Okumoto of Studio3

Caroline E. Sakai, PhD, is a clinical psychologist and social worker in private practice. She is retired from Kaiser Hawaii Behavioral Health Services, where she was chief psychologist and served for 31 years. She works with adults and children with problems ranging from stress, anxiety, depression, and anger to relationship issues, pain, and health concerns. Caroline has worked extensively with traumatic memories both in clinical practice and in work in the field with large-scale trauma, and has been deployed on trauma-relief missions to New Orleans and Rwanda. She has presented at international conferences and published articles on Thought Field Therapy, EMDR, and domestic violence. Caroline also conducts trainings and workshops. For further information, visit her website: www.tftcenter.com